INFLUENCE
ON PURPOSE

PALMETTO

P U B L I S H I N G

Charleston, SC

www.PalmettoPublishing.com

Hardcover ISBN: 979-8-8229-4296-7

Paperback ISBN: 979-8-8229-4297-4

eBook ISBN: 979-8-8229-4298-1

5 PRINCIPLES FOR LEADERS TO BUILD REGENERATIVE CULTURES

INFLUENCE ON PURPOSE

JOHN BAKER

WITH COMMENTS FROM REBEKAH EYRE

If you are looking for a book that will take you on a journey to finding the key to success in building and maintaining your culture in the correct way, I would highly recommend John's book! The way in which the content was presented made it very easy to read and understand. In addition, the real-life examples shared throughout the book brought the principles to life, helping the reader further understand the content being presented. Overall, I am very excited to apply the valuable information shared to build a regenerative culture within my team and Company!

Ashley Pittenger, President
Foster Logistics, Robinson Investments

"......a thought-provoking, highly logical and enjoyable read – John has captured the essence of why nurturing and growing our organisational culture is so critical for long-term success - in this book he provides the tools and know-how to help Leaders do exactly that!"

Gary Crawford, Executive Vice President
TRC

I highly recommend the book "Influence on Purpose: Five Principles for Leaders to Build Regenerative Culture" by John Baker and Rebekah Eyre. Having John work with me over the years as an executive coach and providing leadership training at our company, I can attest to the transformative impact these principles have on organizational culture.

John and Rebekah distill years of experience and research into these essential principles that empower leaders to drive positive change within their organizations. Grounded in real-world examples and authored by someone with a deep understanding of our company's journey, this book serves as a practical guide for leaders committed to creating lasting positive change. It is a must-read for anyone aspiring to foster regenerative cultures and I will share this book across our team.

These principles are also applicable to our personal lives outside of the corporate environment and John and Rebekah use real life and often entertaining examples of when those principles were implemented successfully as well as the times when they were not. Improve your own leadership skills and create a truly regenerative culture at your company by examining how you apply the 5 principles detailed in this book in your professional and personal lives.

Phillip Wenzell, Vice President, Strategy and Corporate Development
Allied Mineral Products

John and Rebekah have captured the essence of having a successful enterprise for the long term. Constant investment in your principles and values should be a natural conclusion and habit of any leader. The environment must stay fertile and healthy to ensure success. Regenerative thinking defines the platform for sustainable growth.

Jon R. Tabor, Chairman and Chief Executive Officer
Allied Mineral Products, Inc.

"John and Rebekah have masterfully tackled the dynamics of organizational culture through the introduction of a model that delivers a clear method that will empower and strengthen leaders to make real and sustainable change in their organizations! Any serious change agent and leader should make this book a staple resource as they work towards success in their organization."

David Boss, PhD Professor of Business Strategy and Leadership,
Motivational Speaker, Business Owner

"I have enjoyed knowing and working with John for over two decades. This book succinctly delivers years of wisdom in an easy-to-consume format. The lessons in this book can set any leader to upgrade their capability to lead and drive sustainable change through their culture."

RJ Nicolosi
President and Chief People Officer Infillion

"The concepts of regenerative leadership and regenerative culture are timely and significant. For reasons not yet fully understood, employees are coming to work even more stressed and less resilient than in the past. We have not recovered from social and environmental impacts coincident to COVID. That our organizations can be a source of life, vitality and added resilience in peoples' lives is powerful and significant. There is no reason to believe that outside pressures and stresses will decrease anytime soon. To create a culture that contributes to healing and vitality, rather than simply reducing potential damage, is a significant step forward. The down-to-earth writing style, seasoned wisdom, and clear illustrative stories make this book inviting as well as compelling."

Dr. David H. Campbell, PhD
Personal Vision 360 Executive Coaching

A Must-Read for leaders looking to regenerate their culture with the right purpose and principles that enable high growth, employee engagement and productivity.

Beth Thomas,
Author of Powered by Happy, Founder /
CEO of Change4Growth, Partner ISG

ACKNOWLEDGEMENTS

This book is largely our striving to understand the principles that apply to all organizations. We acknowledge that principles come from God. We don't claim to have created them or to own them. We do our best to discover and work from eternal principles.

I am grateful to and for my family. I am grateful for Margot who I am blessed to be married to. Our partnership in creating the culture of our family has been and continues to be the greatest work I've been honored to participate in.

I am grateful for the many colleagues, clients and friends who have helped to shape my understanding of the principles. I am grateful for inspired, dedicated leaders who I have had the privilege of serving as an executive coach. They have taught me much as we have worked together to understand stewardship and create regenerative cultures.

TABLE OF CONTENTS

INTRODUCTION FROM JOHN

By way of personal introduction, I am an executive and leadership coach by vocation. I am a rancher by avocation. I use the terms avocation and vocation somewhat tentatively. Vocation generally means what you do for work, avocation usually refers to recreation or non-work, interest-based activity. What makes these terms questionable for me is: I truly enjoy and feel called to help people become the leaders they want to be, for their sake as well as for the benefit of their stakeholders. I am a rancher by choice but it's a lot of hard work; demanding, uncompromising, work.

I have worked with leaders and organizational culture for decades now, it is how I've earned my living. I've worked with livestock for that long as well. Mostly on a small scale. It's how I've chosen to raise my family.

You would think those two occupations (how I occupy myself) couldn't be further apart. Well, here's the thing: I have found many benefits because of the intersection and juxtaposition of organizational leadership and ranching. (Full disclosure, I have studied and practiced leadership coaching and organizational consulting professionally for many years. Though there is always more to learn, I am considered a professional or an expert in this field. I have also been raising livestock for as many years... even with a goal toward creating a profitable ranch/business. However, in this field I consider myself very much a novice.) These two perspectives help me to understand the absolute role and value of Principle. Please understand, I use the term 'absolute' purposefully and very rarely.

These two perspectives help me understand the fundamental role of principle the way an accountant understands and trusts the bottom line of a spreadsheet. When the rows and the columns both add up to the same number you can trust the outcome. Two perspectives arriving at the same conclusion.

So here is where we get to the point I really want to make. The highest level of accomplishment in both settings (any setting including family) is one of creating a regenerative culture. You've no doubt heard the term sustainable referring to a desired state applied to both business and agriculture. Sustainable would be fine if there is no room for improvement. The industrial age has brought many benefits in terms of efficiency, innovation, and wealth. Unfortunately, this has come at an incredibly high cost when applied to both people and the environment. This is mostly because both industrialized business and industrialized agriculture is a mining process extracting without renewing. Mining any living organism or system leads to degeneration, whether we're talking about the fertility of our soil in agriculture or the health and vitality of an organizational culture (the alignment and engagement of people in the service of a mission). When natural resources are exploited, we end up with ecological depletion. When people are exploited, we end up with burnout. Lest you think I'm being too harsh; exploitation is seldom intended. It is usually an unintended consequence of shortsighted management of living resources be they ecological or human. Regenerative is not only sustainable, it is both healing and renewing.

Walt Davis, author, agricultural consultant, and rancher explained two very important points. 1: All agriculture, ranching included, is a biological rather than an industrial process. 2: Ranch profitability and sustainability is best accomplished when the complex relationships of the living organisms involved are managed to mimic how they were created and maintained prior to human intervention. (Paraphrased from "Critical

Knowledge for Ranchers" 10 July 2017.) These are powerful points that apply to leadership of organizations. To apply these two points for our perspective: 1, Culture is biological not industrial. 2, Success is dependent on the quality of relationships between all stakeholders. An initial consideration to being a leader who creates a regenerative culture is to understand the concept of stewardship rather than industrialization.

I've created two organizations for which I currently have stewardship. Homecoming Ranch is all about healing the land and producing healthy nutritionally dense food through regenerative ranching. Influence On Purpose is all about creating healing, successful organizational cultures through regenerative leadership. Both are based on an understanding of principle and require specific character traits.

Principle is defined as a fundamental truth or proposition that serves as a foundation for a system of belief or behavior or for a chain of reasoning. There are governing principles that provide the foundation for sustainable success in any area. Examples are the principles of flight, corporate principles, and principles of regenerative agriculture. In this book, we'll identify the governing principles of leadership required to create a regenerative culture in your organization.

In talking with a friend and colleague, we discussed strategies for building our practices. I shared with him part of our model for leadership influence on building regenerative cultures. As we talked of the principles common in both organizational and agricultural models, he said "John, I think that's your differentiator. Who else can talk about regenerative cultures from both perspectives?"

So, there you have it. Our work is to help you build a regenerative culture that will allow you to achieve greater results by strengthening organizational integrity through effective leadership. These are the principles evident in Jim Collins' "Flywheel" and Malcolm Gladwell's "Tipping point" among others. These are not my principles, no one can legitimately claim to own them or to have created them. They were created by God (or the universe if that makes you more comfortable). We just work to identify them and understand them. We build models, plans, and practices that are rooted in these principles. When we do so successfully, the cultures we create take on a life of their own. Energy is created not depleted. We set ourselves up to lead in ways that develop people and create results.

In this book, we will identify a model that illustrates a regenerative culture. We'll explore each area of that model. You'll learn working definitions of commonly misinterpreted terms. You'll see the fundamental components required to build a culture of integrity. We'll identify the principles and character traits that make the difference between a culture that depletes its living resources and a culture that adds life and energy over time. We also identify the counterfeit principles and character traits that can fool us into thinking we are building a sustainable culture. We will share a process and a tool that will help you build a high trust relationship with each of your stakeholders as individuals rather than categories.

Influence On Purpose is a principle driven practice made of models and processes designed to help leaders create regenerative cultures for themselves and their stakeholders. If more farmers and ranchers would practice regenerative agriculture, it would heal the planet. If more leaders would cultivate regenerative organizations, it would heal our society.

John,
Influence On Purpose

INTRODUCTION FROM REBEKAH

I learned at an early age what a paradigm shift is. While other families might have talked about baseball or school around the dinner table, we learned that an airplane is on track only three percent of the time, but somehow it (almost) always makes it to its destination. We learned about correction, specifically self-correction, about the difference between influence and control, and about how to doctor a goat with sunstroke, all around the family dinner table.

I don't mean to say that my family was perfect or special, or that my parents didn't make mistakes. Of course, they did. But my point is that my father didn't just discover these principles by accident: he lived them. And he taught them, by example as well as by admonition.

I joined the Marine Corps at 18 and served for 10 years, so much of my adult experience with leadership came from the Marines. While some of the practices aren't applicable in the civilian world (good luck assigning your employees extra duties when they mess up) and some of the language certainly isn't, the principles remain the same. They're recognizable in good leaders everywhere, and the lack of principle is recognizable in poor leaders, no matter their title or rank.

At the end of boot camp, my senior drill instructor told my parents, "Usually boot camp is to break the recruits down and then build them up the right way, but we didn't have to do that with Baker. Baker just got it from the beginning." I wasn't a super athlete, and my parents didn't raise us with screaming and push-ups; I was an average marksman and my fitness score was only moderately high. What I "got" from the beginning, what I went to bootcamp with, was an understanding of hard work and of consequences; I understood what I could control and what I couldn't.

What I understood, in so many words, was the Law of the Harvest. I understood what I could influence and what I couldn't, and if I couldn't influence it, I knew I had to let it go. And despite the physical and mental hardships, boot camp is really very simple: do what you're told.

There were similar moments throughout the Marine Corps where I recognized principles at work, even if I didn't always realize it at the time. Looking back, it's easier to point out the principles at play and the lack of them. There were leaders who, while I liked them personally and got along with them, didn't do a good job of developing their Marines, who resorted to fear or anger as motivators instead of digging deeper. There were officers who gave vague directions and were then angry when they didn't get the results they wanted. There were good people, good Marines, who were only average leaders because they didn't know the principles.

The best leader I had the pleasure to work with was nothing like me: a middle-aged, divorced, crusty officer with a taste for whisky and Sweet-tarts. But he was the best example of a leader I can call to mind in the Marine Corps: he "got it." He understood how to develop his Marines, how to rely on principle rather than emotion, even how to be compassionate (in a crusty, Marine sort of way), and how to hold Marines accountable even when it was unpopular or inconvenient.

Similarly, the principles apply outside of the work zone: that's how we know they're true. While interviewing individuals Dad has worked with over the years, I heard again and again how learning with Dad not only improved their business or careers, but their personal and family lives as well. That's when I realized how worthwhile this work really is and how grateful I am to play a part in sharing it with others.

Rebekah D. Eyre
Influence On Purpose

THE SIGNIFICANCE OF A NAME

Our name is derived from two fundamental concepts that guide the work we do in helping leaders achieve their next level of success.

Influence: One of the primary rules of leadership is knowing the difference between control and influence. A leader who expects to control others in any way is destined to fail before they even start. This is manifest in many ways including micro-management, command and control style, manipulation, expecting compensation to drive behavior, etc. This is always a source of frustration and often why leaders get stuck.

When it comes to our impact on outcomes through others, all we have is influence. Leadership coaching is largely a matter of identifying and acting on effective influence strategies. These can be behavioral, systemic or symbolic.

"On Purpose" has two meanings; this is deliberate:

First, 'on purpose' means to be mission focused.

Sustainable success as an individual or an organization is based on rooting core values in sound principles, a compelling vision that is motivating to all, and a mission that addresses the needs and expectations of all stakeholders. Having a well-defined mission provides the transition from aspiration to strategy.

Mission is another word for purpose. So, "Influence On Purpose" means to lead others in a way that helps them align with and engage in the mission of the company.

Second, 'on purpose' means deliberate or intentional.

This meaning addresses another consistent source of frustration for leaders. Most people aren't sufficiently aware that they are always influencing those around them or what that influence contributes to. Too often influence is accidental or happenstance.

"Influence On Purpose" means to be purposeful about your influence. Or to be aware of the effect you are having on others.

The name of the company helps to describe the reason for and the impact of the work we do. Helping leaders identify effective influence strategies that align the efforts of their associates with the mission of the organization is at the core of creating a successful culture.

We help you to Influence On Purpose.

CHAPTER 1

PRACTICES

PLAN

MISSION

VISION

VALUES

PRINCIPLES

9

THE LIVING TREE MODEL

Many years ago, I was watching a presentation given by a mentor of mine. He was explaining the crucial role of values, vision, and mission as a foundation for the strategic planning process. On a flip chart he drew a diagram of a triangle with three levels. In this way he explained how values provide a structural foundation, vision is built on values, and mission was a strategic expression of the vision.

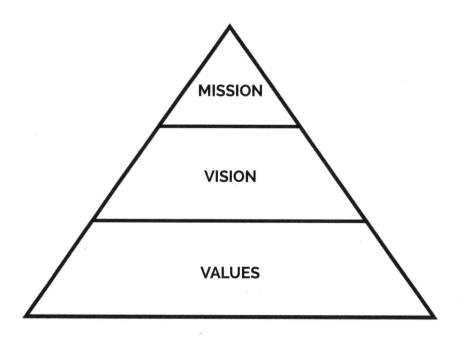

As I watched the presentation from the back of the room, I got a different picture. I saw organizations as growing, living things. I drew a rough picture in my notes that looked something like this:

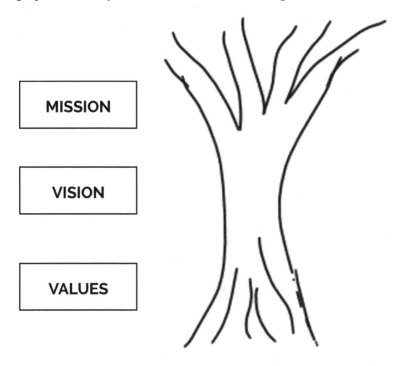

MISSION

VISION

VALUES

If you use your imagination, you may be able to see I was picturing a tree. In the model I show how values bring life into the organization, vision brings unity and direction, and mission is the work of identifying and understanding the needs of the stakeholders.

The roots represent values. These provide the anchor for the organization. They are non-negotiable. They not only provide the foundation for your business; they shape how you live your life. I came to define values as: *Principle centered ideals by which you measure the worth of actions, interactions, and outcomes.*

The trunk of the tree represents vision. As you look to the future, how will the organization be described? This is the challenge to become. The company's vision is that compelling picture that makes the work worthwhile. As the leader expresses the vision, associates can see and determine for themselves if this is work they want to be engaged in. The definition of vision is: *The desired reality to come.*

The mission is a clear statement of what is required for all stakeholders if you are to accomplish the vision. A mission should take into consideration, customers, employees, owners/investors, business partners and or vendors, and the community. A mission that only recognizes one stakeholder group will not be sustainable. Mission is defined as: *the shared purpose that serves all stakeholders.*

A well-defined mission provides the transition from aspirational to strategic. Over the years, the model expanded to show the strategic process more clearly. From the main branches of the tree, secondary and tertiary branches continue. **The secondary branches represent the plans** created to serve the needs of the stakeholders they extend from. Likewise, **the tertiary branches represent the practices** developed to execute those plans.

Unlike the values represented by the roots, plans and practices are very negotiable. Where the roots become permanent and provide consistent nourishment over time, the branches can and should be pruned regularly.

The significance of this model goes beyond typical strategic planning. Fully understood, the model provides a way to plan and grow the culture you need to accomplish your mission.

One day I was explaining the model to a client. I told him he could think of the culture of his company similar to the use of the word in the terms horticulture or agriculture. Leaders can cultivate and nurture a culture perfectly designed to get the results they need to accomplish their goals and sustain their success. He suggested the term "busni-culture." I'm not sure if the term will catch on, I knew he got the picture.

When I knew I wanted the tree to be a logo for my business, I found a clip art version that served the purpose of showing all the components of the model.

What Was Missing

Over time, I came to understand the model gives a good description of an organization's unique culture. Leaders feel empowered knowing culture is definable and is something they can influence. However, there was something in the early years I hadn't gotten a handle on.

As I have worked with a variety of organizations and individuals, I've come to notice they have both unique differences and common traits. The tree in the model effectively represents the organization. However, just as a tree needs to be rooted in rich soil to receive the nourishment it needs to grow, each organization needs values that draw from sound principles to gain and sustain vitality.

Many years ago, in a meeting with a CEO, our conversation included a discussion about core values. I explained there is a difference between values and principles. Values are unique to the individual or organization as described above. Principles exist outside of the individual or organization. The ability for an organization to become regenerative is largely determined by how well their values are rooted in sound principle.

This CEO stopped and pondered. He said, "I'll have to think about that." He, like many others, thought of values and principles as meaning essentially the same thing. It's easy to see values as the absolute foundation when you don't see beyond the boundaries of your own organization. Or as we'll soon discuss, your own reality. Principle is defined as "A fundamental truth or proposition that serves as a foundation for a system of beliefs or behavior or for a chain of reasoning." Oxford Dictionary. These can also be understood as governing principles. As in the governing principles of flight, the governing principles of thermodynamics, or the governing principles of regenerative agriculture. I believe there are governing principles of regenerative human cultures.

It's important to understand the difference between values and principles. Our values, in and of themselves can be constructive, neutral, or destructive, depending on our character and how we express our values as people and organizations. For example, the value of honesty founded in pride can take you no further than your own reality: what you believe to be true, limited to your own perspective. Honesty motivated by humility can lead you closer to the truth as you try to incorporate the perspectives of others into your reality. Honesty motivated by arrogance or selfishness (pride) is constrictive. With the character of pride, you will not be able to see beyond your own perspective. This restricts your reality and will cause it to be inaccurate. Honesty is the value; pride and humility are character traits. Individual reality is the counterfeit of the principle. Truth is the principle.

In other words, for the value of honesty to prove a regenerative source of nourishment to your organization, it must be rooted in the principle of truth. Like all principles, truth is not subject to interpretation or negotiation: it simply is, existing beyond limited points of view. It is our responsibility to bring our viewpoints as close as possible to it. You will not get to the truth if your pride (character) will not allow you to see beyond your own perspective (reality).

There are five principles identified as common to any organization or individual regardless of age, race, gender, region or country. The above example points out **truth** as one of those principles. The other four are **the law of the harvest, agency, love,** and **creation.** Though they may be expressed very differently, these five principles are present in and important to any successful organization around the world. To the degree they can be identified and nourished, any culture can be strengthened and become regenerative.

Overall, the organizational model of the tree represents the ability to cultivate life and vitality in your organization.

This model has consistently served to help leaders develop a plan for their organizations and act on the culture they needed to succeed. The more I did this work, the more I felt the model needed to be an expression of life and vitality. I also came to understand the importance of the soil and not just a tree suspended in air.

Look back at the triangle model of values, vision, and mission. The hard lines of the structure make it look self-contained with no need for, or acknowledgement of, outside forces. Look now at the model of the tree. The model reaches down for strength and security, it reaches up for growth and expression. Reaching down it finds life-giving strength and stability in sound principles. Reaching out it experiences growth and bears fruit in serving stakeholders.

Fortunately, I have a daughter who is a wonderful artist. I called her and described this model and how I use it to help leaders build the organizational culture they need. I asked her if she could paint a picture of the tree. In addition to the tree itself, I asked her to show the soil as a rich and necessary part of the picture. Below is the painting she created. I couldn't be more pleased. It shows the health and vitality of the tree in all its parts. It also shows the richness of the soil.

With the help of clients, mentors, advisors, my daughter's artistic vision, and a very talented friend who helped me see my business from a marketing perspective, that early sketch has become a powerful model for organizational culture.

Who is this book for?

I work with successful people who want to succeed on another level. Everyone I work with has already achieved a position of responsibility. They find they've earned the opportunity to hit an obstacle or overcome a barrier they would never have reached if they had not succeeded to that point. I help people to develop leadership skills and organizations based in principles that produce trusting relationships. These perspectives and skills help them expand their influence and develop regenerative cultures.

Many leaders are faced with the challenge of taking their organizations to another level. This transition comes in many forms, such as an entrepreneur who has successfully taken the company to a point that will require a team of leaders to continue to progress; a family business that has been around for years that must hand it off to the next generation; or a company that exists successfully in its market and sees opportunity in a larger or expanded market.

This is where organizations often hit a wall. The problem, as with individual career development, is the behaviors that created success at one level all but guarantee failure at the next.

For example, as entrepreneurs drive their business to success, they should turn a blind eye and deaf ear to all those who say it cannot be done. They must be aware of all the obstacles facing the fledgling organization and overcome them, often through sheer determination. As the organizations grow, however, their capacity is reached, and they become a bottleneck. The tactics that bring an organization to life become the behaviors that stunt their growth.

Rebekah: Shortly after I reenlisted in the Marine Corps, I was promoted from Sergeant to Staff Sergeant. This meant I became a Staff Non-commissioned Officer, with new responsibilities, duties, and expectations to meet. My 1st Sergeant, the senior enlisted man in my company, gave a book to me and to every other Staff NCO who had recently been promoted: What Got You Here Won't Get You There, by Marshall Goldsmith. He called us all together to discuss why he had invested his own money in getting us these books. He explained that, so far, we had succeeded as Marines. We had successfully fulfilled our duties and roles in our previous ranks and positions. But from now on, to continue succeeding, we would have to change. We would have to grow. Thus far, I had been successful as a Lance Corporal, a Corporal, a Sergeant, simply by following orders. It hadn't always been easy, but it had been simple. As a Staff NCO, he explained, just doing as I was told was no longer going to be enough. Just doing what I was told would make me a very poor leader.

By definition, growth requires change. This book is for leaders who are asking questions like "What direction are we going? Am I thinking strategically? Am I just getting the job done or am I being innovative?" "How do I go from managing people's performance to developing other leaders?" The people who are going to benefit from this book are going to be those who are ready to learn, who don't have what Nelson Nash called "Arrival Syndrome." In other words, "I have arrived, there's nothing more to learn." For so many leaders, arrogance or pride is the number one reason for failure.

This book is for leaders who want to be better leaders, who want to find a voice, to have difficult conversations that are productive instead of hostile. I worked with one young woman who was a high potential manager that the company executives felt would be a future leader in the company, and she felt the concepts she learned in our coaching sessions helped her to have conversations that she was avoiding before. In many cases, she felt she didn't even know what conversations to have and if she did recognize important issues, she thought they were just so sensitive she didn't know how to bring them up. Now, she's having conversations that she was afraid to have, even up three or four levels of leadership. Some of the senior executives are now recognizing her contributions where she used to feel invisible.

She felt learning to be a better leader, and the concepts that she learned to help her grow as a leader, helped her find her voice. She said what's next for her is to think about the tree and what does her personal one look like, what are her own core values? Recognizing principles will help shape her career going forward. She feels now that she has a career, not just a job.

This book is for leaders who know that culture matters. Peter Drucker famously said, "Culture eats strategy for breakfast." No matter how detailed, intricate, or brilliant your strategy and tactical plans are, they will not compensate for a declining or degenerative culture. Culture is a result of the values you live, it's *what you do*, no matter what it says on your wall or letterhead. Regenerative culture is the result of being rooted in principles, of living your values and vision, of being focused on your mission. Leaders we've spoken with credit their positive outcomes to a great culture: it's why employees enjoy coming to work, why one client boasts a below-average turnover rate for his industry, why another has excellent relationships with vendors and customers. Your culture will determine your results.

Another purpose of this book is to make the principles we teach more accessible. One emerging leader said a book would not only help him to remember some of the techniques, principles and perspectives we discussed, it would also help to teach others. If he wants to explain the point, he can say "Hey, look at this book; let's go through it together" rather than having to translate it into his own words and feeling like he lost something in translation.

Why we start with the soil

In a cultural assessment I conducted for a client, one of the things I noted is that they defined culture and business outcomes as completely different areas of focus. Business was the hard stuff and culture was the soft stuff, which is unfortunate. Culture drives it all, it's all culture. How you do business, what you decide is going to be your profit margin, that's all part of your culture. When people try to define business and culture as two separate things, what they do is diminish the reality of culture, they'll relegate what they say is the soft side of the business as less important. But that's where you find quality of relationships, trust, what we do, how we do it and why, all the things that actually drive business outcomes, that make them most predictable and most successful. Culture gets shunted, and then people don't understand why they aren't getting the outcomes they want even though they're focusing on what they think are the most important things. In this very company, the CEO gets very impatient if you really take the time to try to define the mission so you can communicate it better. "People just need to do their jobs. I don't have time for that."

The drivers of our business cultures are so often the things that don't get measured, that are invisible. Adherence to a mission, clearly defined and relevant values, and understanding that at the root of it all are principles that make your business regenerative.

When you understand how your culture is created, you can influence it. The danger to your business comes when you don't understand your culture, when you don't see what's driving it. You don't have to step in the trap if you know it's there. It's the trap you don't see that gets you every time. It's making the invisible visible that really empowers people in their culture.

The entire tree model represents culture, starting with principles, going all the way up through outcomes. The fruit on the tree is based on how well you cultivated that tree. If your fruit is not what you want and you're really frustrated, you're probably missing something. When cultivating your "busni-culture," as any regenerative farmer or rancher will tell you, you have to start with the soil. Everything starts with the principles.

CHAPTER 2

PRACTICES

PLAN

MISSION

VISION

VALUES

PRINCIPLES

THE PRINCIPLES OF A
REGENERATIVE CULTURE

Overall, the organizational model of the tree represents the ability to cultivate life and vitality in your organization. Over time this model served to help leaders develop a vision for their organizations and act on the culture they needed to succeed. The more I did this work, the more I felt the model needed to be an expression of life and vitality. I also came to understand the importance of the soil and not just a tree suspended in air.

The model we use emerged first as seeing culture as organic (a living thing, always growing or dying) rather than inert building blocks. For me, that was the first breakthrough. Not in what culture is, rather how culture is represented. I've worked with many leaders who resist talking about values, vision, and mission because in the past they've found it to be fruitless (pun intended). They could not find a way to progress from words on paper that sounded right to actionable plans and practices that garnered employee buy-in. However, when they used this model to represent their organizations, they found they were able to move forward with sustainable business strategies that were well integrated with why the business existed in the first place. The outcomes of the business are directly connected and affected by the values at the root of the organization. In upcoming chapters we'll walk through those steps.

First, we start with the soil. Starting with the soil might seem counterintuitive. Most work on organizational culture tends to start with the fruits (i.e., the outcomes) of labor and work backward. Similarly, years ago, ranching used to be about raising as big a cow as possible. In regenerative ranching, we realized you can't raise a healthy cow, profitably, unless you really manage your grasses well, your forage. And then we realized, you can't manage the forage well unless you have healthy soil. And then we realized, you can't have healthy soil unless the microbes, microscopic lifeforms, are healthy and being fed and nurtured. Burke Teichert, an experienced rancher, leader and consultant, among others, wrote a great deal on soil health and even soil life being the basis of a profitable, sustainable ranch.

In many circles, ranching has become synonymous with losing money. Most people will tell you, the only way to make a small fortune in ranching is to start with a large fortune. And yet that's not true when you understand the business of managing the ranch all the way down to the microbes. Think of making the invisible, visible. If you understand what you're dealing with, you can influence it. Your ranching process can feed the soil rather than deplete it. When you go for what you think is that first profit driver, when you focus only on the outcomes, you usually deplete your resources faster than you can replenish them. And yet, if you start with the foundation, meaning you cultivate the soil, the very act of ranching becomes regenerative, you replenish the soil as you are building the herd and the cow.

If you are focused on the principles, if everything you do leads back to and is rooted in those principles, the very act of doing business replenishes the resources needed to nourish and grow your business. This is true of the human relationships we call business. We can work in a way that strengthens and nourishes our relationships over time. These are the organizations that benefit from reputations that maintain valued

relationships and invite new ones. Stakeholders are drawn to these organizations. That's the ideal state, that's regenerative!

That is why this book is organized to walk us through the tree, starting with the soil.

Coming to view the model of an organization as a living entity was
my first breakthrough. The next breakthrough came as I was driving
down the interstate to an appointment with a client. The thought came
to me with such clarity and urgency, I worked my way through three
lanes of traffic to the side of the highway to write it down. The thought
provided clarity on the difference between the nature of values and principles (discussed in chapter one) as well as the role of individual character. Values of themselves can be productive or destructive... depending
on the goals and character of the individual. What I wrote was similar to
this section of chapter one:

*It's important to understand the difference between values and prin-
ciples. Our values, in and of themselves can be constructive, neutral or destructive. For example: The value of honesty based in pride can take you no
further than your own reality (a very limited and possibly dysfunctional
world view). Honesty motivated by humility can lead you to a more accurate reality, better aligned with the truth. Honesty motivated by arrogance
or selfishness (pride) can be destructive. Honesty is the value; pride and humility are character traits; Individual reality is the counterfeit; Truth is
the principle.*

*In other words, for the value of honesty to prove a sustainable source
of nourishment to your organization, it must be rooted in the principle of
truth. You will not get to the truth if your pride will not allow you to see
beyond your own perspective (reality).*

This can be mapped out for each of the five principles as follows:

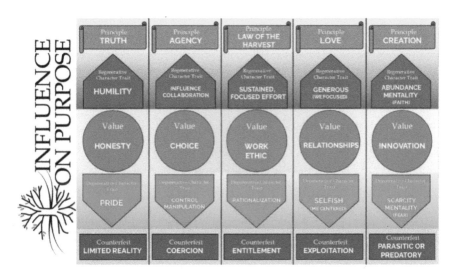

This then is the great news! Understanding the role and importance of values as the root of your culture may help to make your organization sustainable. However, understanding the role and importance of principles in nourishing your culture can make your organization regenerative. Just as successful ranching usually starts with soil analysis, a successful business needs to analyze and understand what brings life and energy to the organization. We will return to this chart later to explain the relationships between principles, values, and character traits and how they impact an organization. It's important first to understand the principles and that growing from them is what creates a regenerative culture. So, what are the principles and where do they come from?

The five identified principles common to any organization or individual regardless of circumstance, religion, country, race, or profession are **truth, law of the harvest, agency, love,** and **creation**. These are the invisible things that must be made visible to nourish the roots, the foundation, of any organization. They are not unique to a specific industry or position. We can take no credit for creating them: they are not man-made concepts or values, but to the extent we seek to recognize, understand, and build from them, they can turn man-made ventures into regenerative organizations.

Principle 1 Truth: the courage and humility to go beyond individual and group realities.

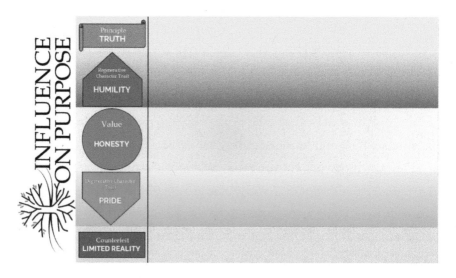

I mentioned in the first chapter an encounter with a CEO: when I commented on a certain negative situation, he said "That's just reality." My response was: "But is it true?" We often hear phrases such as "Speak your truth" or "That's my truth." What we mean, of course, is "Share your perspective" and "That's my reality." Because Truth, with a capital

T, is all encompassing and independent of individual or group perspective. Reality is created through our perceptions. Though perceptions are realities, realities are never completely true and are always incomplete. Increasing the accuracy of our realities can only be achieved through the humility and courage to challenge those realities. Truth is there whether we get it or not. **Realities** are individual creations, truth is **discovered**.

As you'll see, many of the words we use in coaching and in this book are structural in nature, rather than emotional. Truth is not subject to our emotions or perceptions: it is whole and completely accurate. What do I mean by that? When I was young, I worked as a carpenter. If my boss said "Hey, John, pick up that board and before you hand it to me, check and make sure it's true," he wasn't asking me "Is this an honest board who will never lie." It's a piece of wood. What he was asking me to do was look along the length of the board and make sure it wasn't warped. A true board isn't warped or distorted. That's what True means. Our perceptions are distortions of that Truth, distorted fragments. We open ourselves to a process of discovery, including the perspectives of others, to get closer to the standard of Truth. That takes humility and courage.

To draw from another common adage, the saying "There's two sides to every story" is a good example of the difference between reality and truth. Doubtless you've heard two people see or experience the same event but tell very different versions of it. Yet you know that, somewhere, is the truth of an event that actually occurred. The event is the truth; the two stories are simply two perspectives of that event, two realities. If we are willing to understand other people's realities, if we are humble and willing to listen, we will have a more accurate reality that brings us closer to the Truth.

Learning to listen to other's perspectives, to try to integrate the different sides of the story, will get us closer to Truth. You cannot lead someone, and often can't even work well with them, when you have diametrically opposed "truths;" in such a situation the other person will always be wrong, ignorant, arrogant, etc., whatever it is that is keeping them from accepting our "truth." But when we can both accept that our realities are not completely true, we are open to the possibility of understanding other's perspectives, creating opportunities to better communicate and build trust in our relationships with our stakeholders.

Principle 2 Agency: understanding choice and consequences

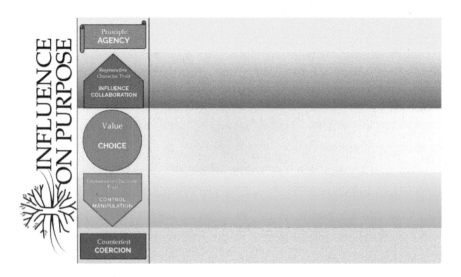

Agency is the ability and privilege to choose and act for ourselves.

As leaders it is important not only to take ownership of our own choices and their consequences, we need to respect that each of our stakeholders (employees, customers, etc.) choose each day to be engaged with us or not to be. Acknowledging agency helps leaders work to influence others and avoid the trap of trying to control. True leadership is about influence, not control. Returning to the ranching metaphor, you can't control the microbes in your soil, but you can influence them with how you manage. You can't control the thoughts and actions of your team members; you can only influence them, and allow theirs to influence you.

In business, as in life, alignment with a specific course and engagement in the work of that cause are choices we make. Choice precedes and largely determines both direction and destination. When you choose a path, you choose the place it leads to. Choice and consequence are infinitely linked: you cannot have one without the other. Steven Covey compared choice and consequence to picking up a stick: you can't pick up one end of the stick without picking up or manipulating the other end in some way, in the same way you cannot fail to do laundry and reasonably expect to have clean clothes. When we can look at the situation we are in and trace it back to the choices we have made, then we have the ability to influence that situation by adjusting our choices accordingly. Obviously, our lives are impacted by the choices of others and by uncontrollable events such as the weather or some diseases, but when we complain about our circumstances but don't address or adjust our own behavior, it demonstrates a complete lack of understanding of the principle of agency.

Rebekah: Growing up, we learned at an early age to never make the mistake of saying "they made me angry" or "I didn't have a choice." Statements like these would elicit kindly lectures from Dad and we quickly learned to say instead "I'm angry" or "I didn't want to" and save ourselves from the speeches. And yet these are often phrases you will hear adults say and believe to be true. But just like we were taught as children, phrases like these deny individual agency and turn us into perpetual victims of circumstance, unable to control our own emotions or actions. What we really mean is that we view something as unreasonable, inappropriate, wrong, whatever it might be that provokes anger and we feel justified in our reaction, in being angry. Or we are faced with an option that is so unpleasant that we don't even consider taking it, such as losing our job or incurring someone's anger. But as my dad used to tell us and I now tell my son: there is always a choice.

Principle 3 Law of the Harvest: applying focused, sustained effort and achieving desired outcomes.

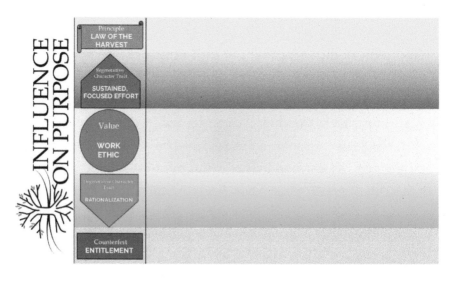

A basic example of the law of the harvest is understanding what is required for the production of fruit. If you want to have an apple, an apple seed must be planted. The soil will need to have sufficient nutrients.

The seed and growing plant will require watering and tending to. As the tree grows, it will need to be nurtured and cared for. As the tree matures it will yield the fruit it is designed to produce. As with our own efforts, many outside factors such as the weather, parasites, or thieves can affect the crop, but the guarantee is that, without work, there will be no harvest.

This principle is so widely recognized that versions of the saying "You reap what you sow" are found in many different cultures and languages. Work is more than just having or doing a job, it is fundamental to any worthwhile accomplishment. Gordon B. Hinckley described work as the "magic by which dreams become reality" and J. Richard Clarke said "We work to earn a living, that is true, but as we toil, let us also remember that we are building a life. Our work determines what that life will be." Our businesses, relationships and even lives do not happen by accident: they are the direct results of the work we do, or don't, put into them.

Principle 4 Love: the power and importance of relationships

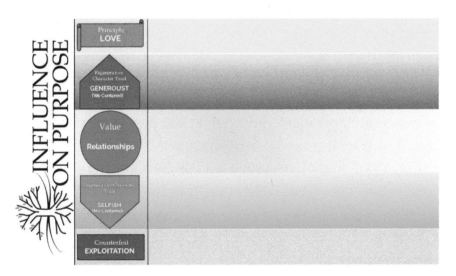

The fourth principle is probably the most powerful, the most uni-fying and the largest determiner of not only achieving but of defining success. This four-letter word is more likely to cause hard-nosed business leaders to squirm with discomfort than any other. However, truly under-standing the principle of love is not a mushy, romantic, or weak position. It instead means recognizing and acknowledging the inherent worth and value of every human being, including ourselves, regardless of gender, race, education, circumstances, or financial achievement. When we truly value each person, we work or interact with, not just for what they can do for us or the organization but because they are human, it will show in our expressions, words, and actions. Can you imagine a world where this won't positively affect relationships between stakeholders?

I find it makes it easier to discuss and to understand when we talk about the common expressions of love in the business environment. Words like civility, respect, forgiveness, and sacrifice are easier to identify in our organizations. It's also easier to see their impact on creating a vital culture and therefore ultimate success. Regardless of the word we use in the moment, the simple fact is that if you do not love others, you are not qualified to lead them. Without respect and compassion, you cannot build the relationships necessary to create a regenerative culture.

I was working with one leader who was constantly expressing anger and frustration with those who reported to her. "They" were always lazy or ignorant. "They" didn't get it and she was tired of them not doing what she wanted them to do. As soon as I noticed this pattern, I realized this wasn't a problem of content, it was a problem of relationship. I told her if you can't find the good in people, you are not qualified to lead them. I've come to see this as a maxim I can trust. Given further thought, I also realized the ability to see good in people has more to do with your character than theirs.

I have noticed for many years and taught my clients: disrespect will always cost you money. Though this is a hard-hitting fact, the cost in dollars is only a small part of the cost when disrespect is expressed or felt. It is important to understand financial loss as a lagging indicator of disrespect. The earlier signs will be loss of alignment and engagement in the form of demoralization or resentment. When people feel disrespected, the driving agenda in their mind is to get back their dignity, usually at the cost of mission accomplishment. This leads to a culture of backbiting, complaining, silos, and even malicious or petty acts of sabotage, all of which take a toll on stakeholder relationships, productivity and inevitably, on profitability. Recognizing and acting on the principle of love in our organizations and relationships is not only the right thing to do, it is the smart thing to do!

Principle 5 Creation: providing value and solutions where none existed.

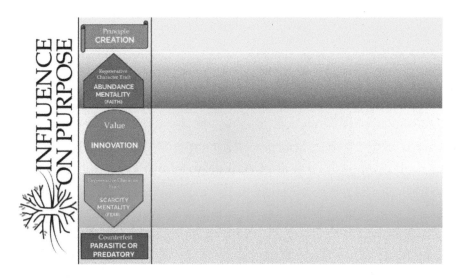

This last principle took me a long time and the help of a close colleague to identify. A friend and I were talking about the first four principles, going through a chart I had organized and making some adjustments or clarifications. As we were looking at this chart, he said "Where would you put innovation as a value? That's an important value at my company."

We had talked about principles before and I had always said, "These are the four I've identified. There are probably more, but these are the ones I know." When he asked about innovation as a value, I couldn't place it on the chart. It didn't seem to fit with the principles I had identified.

He asked where innovation would fit? And as we talked, I realized we had just identified the fifth principle: Creation. In regenerative cultures people create. And there's a difference between creating and just grabbing your piece of the pie. We talked about character traits related to Creation for quite a while, trying to understand it better. What we came to understand was that the principle of Creation is about creating value, or a solution that didn't exist before. We can't create raw materials: we can organize and alter them, but we can't create them. So, to create value you are taking raw materials and adding labor, knowledge, and imagination.

In the book "Crucial Conversations" by Kerry Patterson, Joseph Grenny, Ron McMillan and Al Switzler, they explain, when you find you're at an impasse with another person, one of the best ways to build trust is to have a shared purpose. That's why Mission is the basis for all strategic planning, for all business strategy and that's why the tree is what it is. You must have mission in order to have clear plans and practices that all can even agree on. They teach that, when you have an impasse, it is important to recognize the difference between purpose and strategy, to recognize the purpose behind the strategy. You've got to get to shared purpose to build trust. If you don't have a shared purpose, then you need to invent a mutual purpose. The first time I heard that I thought, "That sounds manipulative. Inventing a mutual purpose, it sounds like Pollyanna: make it up just so we can agree." But then I thought about it again and realized I was wrong. If you think about any real, physical invention, it had to go through a process of taking existing resources and adding value, of creating a solution that hadn't existed before.

At one point in time, there was no cotton gin. All the raw materials for a cotton gin existed, but there was no cotton gin. Eli Whitney figured out how to put all that stuff together in a way that made a cotton gin to meet a need, to create a solution. There was no telephone, until Alexander Graham Bell figured out how to put all that stuff together and channel the electricity; I still don't understand how it works, but someone did. They figured it out. They invented a telephone. A car was invented, an airplane was invented, they didn't exist until they were invented. But all the raw materials existed beforehand. That's how you add value; that's how you create. These inventors had to understand the principles that made these inventions possible... That's innovation.

The principle of Creation is essential to adding value. Creating intellectual or intangible solutions is just as necessary and valid as creating physical solutions or inventions. We create new solutions, come up with new ideas each day to solve even small problems, such as how to get home from work when our usual route is closed, entertaining a fussy baby, or even creating works of art in paintings, sculptures, or music. When we recognize the principle of Creation, we recognize that there is no end to innovation, to growth. We realize we don't have to take from others to have more; someone else's company doesn't have to fail for ours to succeed. There are always more solutions and opportunities because humans are always creating them. Rather than just taking for ourselves, when we create, others benefit as well from a solution that wasn't there before.

I've said it before: these aren't my principles. The principles are there. I have identified five, but as I mentioned, I make no claim that there aren't more: there might be five, seven, or a hundred. But these are the ones I have been able to recognize as I've come to understand their necessity for building a truly successful organization, and even a successful life.

All of these principles are a necessary foundation for a thriving, regenerative culture. You can't elevate one at the expense of the others, and you can't neglect one without negatively affecting your organization. For example, acting on the principle of Love might lead you to view with compassion an employee struggling to fill their part of the mission. Such compassion will reasonably cause a leader to see if this employee needs additional support, training, or even counseling. It might even be necessary to re-evaluate the workload to make sure it is reasonable and fair. However, once these supports have been given, if poor performance continues, protecting this employee from the negative consequences of their choices would violate the principles of Agency and Law of the Harvest and make a mockery of the principle of Love. You move from supporting to enabling, probably at the expense of the mission or other employees who have to pick up the slack. It is possible to respectfully and compassionately give a negative performance review or even let someone go. Principles are mutually reinforcing and cannot be isolated from each other without negative effects.

CHAPTER 3

PRACTICES

PLAN

MISSION

VISION

VALUES

PRINCIPLES

COUNTERFEITS OF PRINCIPLES

Recognizing the Counterfeit

For every principle, there is a counterfeit. Think for a minute about counterfeit money: a fake 20-dollar bill appears very similar to a genuine bill, but it is worthless or even negative in value. Counterfeiting is illegal because it is destructive to a nation's economy; it undervalues the local currency and breeds distrust among the populace.

Counterfeit principles are the same: while they might appear to be genuine and lead to success in the short term, in the long run, they will lead to a culture of mistrust and degeneration. Symptoms of counterfeit principles include greed, damaged relationships, dysfunctional teams, low morale, distrust, and poor reputation. Recognizing these counterfeits for what they are and turning instead to the genuine principles is necessary to build that healthy, growing tree we use in our organizational model.

If we review our Principles Chart, at the bottom we can see the counterfeit of every principle, like a distorted reflection:

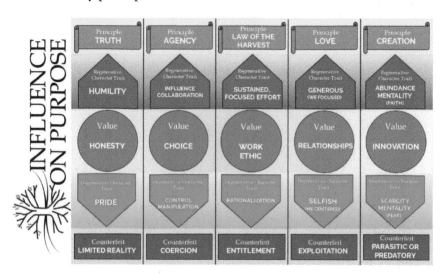

Reality disorder the counterfeit of Truth

The counterfeit of Truth is limited reality or even a reality disorder: when we believe that our perceptions are reality, and that reality is Truth, regardless of other's perceptions or input. These distorted realities are what my friend and mentor Kurt Southam calls "hardening of the categories." Some people just suffer from hardening of the categories, the belief that their reality is true and other perceptions are true only if they agree with their reality. In order to find Truth, you have to have humility because you've got to recognize that reality, by definition, is not Truth. Most of us will suffer from hardening of the categories to varying degrees at different points in our lives. We have to consciously choose to look beyond our reality in order to find Truth. If we never challenge our realities, we're at high risk of suffering from a reality disorder. In daily life, that might look like lack of confidence, it might look like arrogance, it might look like just social awkwardness. There are a lot of things that might look like where we can still function in society or at work. If our reality gets too far away from what is True, then it starts to become dysfunctional and disruptive. It can become debilitating addiction, mental illness, deep depression. As we have the humility to challenge our realities with confidence that there is a Truth, we move further from the counterfeit and closer to the principle.

Coercion the counterfeit of Agency

Coercion is the counterfeit of Agency. This comes from the character traits of control or manipulation. Ironically, many seem to think that the best leaders are the ones who have the greatest control over their employees or people (they manage their people well). Yet the truth is that the only person we have any hope of controlling is ourselves. With everyone else, all we have is influence. Another thing Kurt taught me early in my career is: "Leadership is what people do when you're not there." When we try to control another person, through incentives, punishments, or manipulation, most often we get the opposite of what we really want, if what we really want is a regenerative culture and trusting relationships.

A story about the Church of Jesus Christ of Latter-day Saints leader, Joseph Smith, perfectly illustrates the difference between Agency and control. John Taylor, the third president of the Church, reported hearing a member of the Illinois legislature ask Joseph Smith how he was able to govern so many people with such good order, adding that it was impossible for them (the legislature) to do it anywhere else. Joseph, in one of the most brilliant leadership quotes I've ever heard, replied he didn't govern them: "I teach them correct principles, and they govern themselves." (John Taylor, "The Organization of the Church," *Millennial Star*, Nov. 15, 1851, p. 339.) With a true understanding of the principle of Agency, it is easier to understand the difference between influence, the effect we have on others, and the desire to control them, to force them to use their agency in a way we direct. Stephen Covey calls this the difference between the Circle of Influence and the Circle of Concern: what we can actually control and what we can't but want to.

Entitlement the counterfeit of The Law of the Harvest

The counterfeit of The Law of the Harvest is entitlement, the notion that we deserve certain things, regardless of any effort on our part. This is often characterized by the phrase "It's not fair" and accompanies feelings of envy, jealousy, or covetousness. This is when we rationalize instead of put forth sustained, focused effort (work ethic). We feel entitled to something someone else has because it's not fair that they have it and we don't. It can also manifest as laziness or lack of accountability: you see this in people who are very good at getting out of work, who consistently fail to deliver on assignments or agreements. Yet, when called out on their behavior, they always have a very good reason why they couldn't accomplish what they were supposed to accomplish. This is the organizational culture where no one goes above and beyond, where the primary goal seems to be to do as little as possible or even no real work at all and get as much in return as possible. There is no comprehension or acknowledgement of value provided or received, of relationships built on trust, or even of the long-term outcomes of such attitudes, which will always be negative.

Rebekah: A good friend of mine works for a company where most, if not all, of the hourly employees are members of a union. Unfortunately, and from what I understand, not uncommonly, these positions of Union and Company often set up a situation of conflict, exploitation, and entitlement. Every few years, the union votes on a contract that details the wages, working conditions, hours, and benefits of the hourly employees. And every time a contract comes up for a vote, there are people who will vote no "on principle." One man's exact words were "I always vote no on principle because I figure we can always get more." And he was not the only one to express similar feelings or display a similar attitude. There was no discussion of the value the employees provide, the obligations of the company to ensure fair compensation and the well-being of employees while at work. This attitude doesn't even consider what might be legitimate complaints against the company or salaried (non-union) employees, such as dishonesty, unsafe working conditions, or below market-value wages. At least on the part of some, the ruling idea is entitlement and greed.

Exploitation the counterfeit of Love

Exploitation is the opposite of Love. To love another human is to recognize that they, like us, have inherent value, regardless of ability level, affinity, or how similar they might be or not be to us. When you recognize this, the natural result is that you treat others justly while still considering your own wants and needs. You look for win-win situations, rather than win at all costs. When you lack this understanding, you view people as objects: you value them only in relation to yourself, in considering what they can do for you, or if they are a part of your group or "other." This is often at work in companies with high turnover, employee abuse, and where people feel they are being used or manipulated.

In The Arbinger Institute's book, "Leadership and Self-Deception: Getting out of the Box," they give the example of employee's reaction to two different leaders: both leaders ask questions about the employee's family, appear to listen to the answers and respond, yet in one case the employee feels the concern is genuine and in the other he feels like he's being "smoothed." In the second case, the leader is asking the right questions and doing the right things, but the employee still feels as if the leader doesn't really care, as if he read a book about "How to be a Good Listener" and was simply following the steps. As you can imagine, the employee's reactions to these two people were markedly different: in the case where he felt his leader actually cared, he was more willing to sacrifice for the team and to take criticism. In the second case, where he felt manipulated or "smoothed," the reaction was entirely negative and cynical. Manipulation stops working as soon as it becomes evident. Even when control tactics seem to get you what you want, they produce only in the short-term and at an unacceptably high cost.

Predation or Parasitism are counterfeits of Creation.

When we talk about Creation, we are talking about adding value to raw materials, creating new solutions to problems that benefit others as well as ourselves. Steven Covey's famous win/win solutions require creativity or innovation. The opposite of that is predation or parasitism: grabbing, covetous, and predatory. This counterfeit doesn't view the world with an abundance mindset, where there is plenty for all and room for growth. This worldview is very limited and limiting: I will get mine by taking from you. It is a limited-pie view, where taking one piece of the pie limits how many pieces are left for others, and the only way to get ahead is to take.

While the principle of Creation sees that more pies can and are made every day, parasitism and predation sees only the pie that someone else has or might have and wants to take it away or get it first. This counterfeit is often behind business strategies that focus heavily on the competition; the question is often "how can we beat them?" instead of "how can we create more value for our customers?" Whenever you hear someone rationalize a hurtful action with "It's just business" you are seeing a lack of principle that contributes to a depleting culture. This outlook is degenerative instead of regenerative. How can you be regenerative when you look at the world with a predatory eye? It's impossible.

As with principles, counterfeits don't just exist by themselves: they often accompany and even cause other counterfeits. For example, knowledge that you are being exploited can trigger feelings of entitlement.

Hardened categories make win-win solutions impossible as you try to control and manipulate others to get them to see things your way. Predatory business practices engender predation and covetousness in others, especially in a company's own stakeholders because they are the first victims. Simon Sinek said, "People don't buy what you do, they buy why you do it." If your company's goal is really to crush the competition, if the strategy is to exploit stakeholders (including customers), it will repel the very stakeholders and deplete the relationships an organization needs to survive and thrive.

Rebekah: Returning to the story of my friend's workplace, many of the union workers who vote no to contracts "on principle" are what are known as "old-timers:" workers who have been there for years, even decades. And they have long memories. They remember when contracts were broken by the company, when promises were extended and then withdrawn. They remember when the company asked for concessions from the hourly workers during times of recession or economic slowdowns, but when those concessions were granted, the company fought or refused to repay those concessions during economic booms, as they had promised. So, the feeling that the Company is only out for what it can get, at the expense of its employees, in turn creates feelings of mistrust, skepticism, entitlement and even predation in its workers: I'll get what I can while I can; it's us versus them. Everyone is fixed in their own realities and the categories are hardened. And of course, there are those who benefit from keeping things that way: workers who are only interested in putting in the bare minimum, union lawyers who would be out of a job if the union and company honestly and humbly tried to negotiate a contract that was win-win, and company representatives who view workers as cogs in a wheel instead of as individuals and humans. And everyone has the comfort of feeling that their position is the right one. The company is surviving and even profitable, but at what cost? What are the hidden costs of sacrificing principle? In this company's case, how much more profitable could they be with employees who didn't just do the bare minimum? How much time and effort (and expense) are spent on fighting over contracts? And employees wouldn't feel the need to pay a union to protect them, sacrificing a portion of their paycheck every month, if they didn't feel they were being exploited. And I could go on. Sacrificing principle always comes at a cost.

CHAPTER 4

PRACTICES

PLAN

MISSION

VISION

VALUES

PRINCIPLES

VALUES AND CHARACTER

Values and Character Traits

As described in the previous chapter, principles exist outside of our individual lives and organizational culture. They are. We can work in alignment with principles and experience what Jim Collins calls the "flywheel affect." Our work and culture can gain momentum and energy over time. Or we can work against these principles and create a culture that grinds us and others down over time.

In this chapter we discuss values. These are yours; you own them. They are not limited to the ones we identify. They are the root of your tree. This is where it gets personal. We'll also discuss the character traits that will either bring nourishment and life into your tree (culture) or cause you to mine ever depleting resources.

Values *(Principle centered ideals by which you measure the worth of actions, interactions and outcomes)*

Do they pass the test?
- Would you build any business around this value?
- Would you retain this value even if it became a competitive disadvantage?
- Would you retain this value even if you were not rewarded to do so?
- Do you feel senior management can model and reinforce this value daily?

- Do you see a clear link to your vision and mission?
- Is this value non-negotiable?

The other elements of the chart are Values and Character Traits.

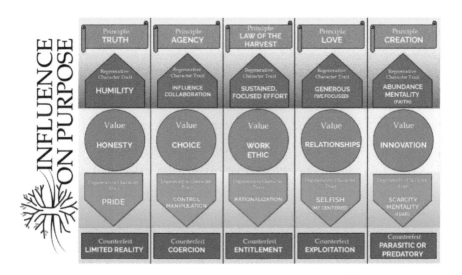

Honesty: Humility vs. Pride

As a prime example, people often say they value honesty. In fact, when we asked people what character traits were necessary for people to succeed at their companies, the very first trait listed was almost invariably honesty. Yet very different people will say they value honesty, and they will get very disparate or dissimilar results. Part of the confusion comes from defining honesty as a character trait. When we define honesty as a value, it allows us to recognize the impact of our character. You can be honest and degenerative or honest and regenerative depending on your character.

We have four children, and I was assigned the role of teaching them to drive, especially when they were first learning how to operate a vehicle. This assignment was given to me by my wife. She told me I had to drive with our children until she knew it was safe to be in the car with them. Not getting the full understanding of her strategy, I asked "does this mean I'm the expendable one?" She quickly explained her perspective. Her concern was if our child started to swerve, run a light or some other inherently dangerous maneuver, she would likely scream, grab the wheel, and exacerbate the situation, with possible deadly results. She went on to explain that I on the other hand would be more likely to calmly redirect or intervene in a way that would preserve the lives of all concerned. A good save, right? Anyway, my ego was spared, and I was blessed with what turned out to be one of my favorite opportunities. These turned out to be priceless one-on-one visits with each of my children.

One such visit was with my oldest daughter. While we were driving Amanda asked me if I thought she was honest. This is one of those situations Rebekah alludes to throughout this book. In my annoying consultant way, I answered her question with a question. "What do you mean by honest?" She said something like: "You know, do you think I'm strait forward, I tell it like it is?" In persistent annoying dad mode, I asked "Do you think that makes you a good communicator?" (I know, I know, many of you are shouting "just answer her &$#@ question you idiot!!!" Hang in there) She said "Yah, I think that makes me a good communicator. Nobody has to guess what I'm thinking." I said, "Well honey, you'd be about half right."

I continued, "let's say I go home and look in your room and find it's not clean and I say: 'Your room is a pigsty, get it cleaned up. As a matter of fact, it's not your room, it's my room, I pay the bills.' How would you feel, what would you do?" She said "first, I'd be really angry, that would be a disrespectful way to talk to me. Next, I'd think of all the times you didn't pick up after yourself." I said, "is your room a mess, should it be clean, do I own the house?" She said, "yah but you shouldn't talk to people that way." To which I heartily agreed.

The moral of the story?... We went on to talk about the purpose of communication. You aren't going to get your message across if your style of delivery damages the person's willingness or ability to understand and receive the message. When my daughter felt disrespected, her focus was on protecting her dignity and defending herself... even if by attacking me. My intended message was totally lost as collateral damage. As explained in the previous chapter: Honesty with the character of pride will lead to miscommunication more often than effective communication. To be effective, honesty requires both caring and courage.

Our oldest daughter has grown up to be one of the most compassionate and courageous people I know. Mostly that's her nature. I like to think that nurture helped support the positive outcome.

As we go through the chart, you can see how values can be associated either with principles or counterfeits *based on our character*. I emphasize this because it is crucial to understanding and applying values profitably in our lives: our character traits lead us to principles or counterfeits, to regeneration or degeneration. For example, for those who say they value honesty, whether they are humble or prideful will make all the difference in their outcomes. People can be honest and wrong, or honest and arrogant, or honest and humble. Humility, the willingness to examine our own realities and be open to the perspectives of others, will bring us closer to Truth. Pride will convince us that our realities are true and don't need examination, against all evidence to the contrary. According to Socrates: The unexamined life is not worth living. My message for my daughter, will your honesty influence others to respond with openness or resistance?

Pride won't let us acknowledge that there are times we shouldn't trust our own reality. When a coworker or spouse angers us, we often tell ourselves stories about the situation to justify our own feelings of anger that don't require any self-reflection or change on our part. I had an experience with this several years ago where I had to pause and question my own reality. It wasn't comfortable but it was necessary. Those who know me know that most of my life I've been pretty 'not wealthy'; as a matter of fact, very not wealthy. So, all of my vehicles, when I was able to get a vehicle, were bought by myself, through my own labor, even as a young man, and they were very often something requiring me to make major repairs such as needing an engine or transmission. They were always fixer-uppers or "beaters."

The first time I bought a vehicle and thought, "Man, I have arrived," was when I purchased a used F250 that didn't have rust on it. It was the first vehicle I ever owned that wasn't rusted. We had four children, and we finally bought a used truck that wasn't rusted. I worked about an hour from home, so I drove the family van with better mileage than the truck, but all week long I was thinking "This weekend, I'm going to work on the barn, I'm going to get the truck, I'm going to go to get some lumber and my son and I are going to build stalls." I had a vision, this was my Saturday, it was all planned.

Finally, Friday came. I had worked over 12 stressful hours that day and I was wiped out. I was driving the family van and I noticed that the tank was pretty low. And I thought, "Eh, there's enough to get home and then enough to get to a gas station, so I'm just going on home." But it was pretty close to empty. Now anybody who grew up in my home will know that 'Dad' always said "Never let the tank get below a quarter. One, it's hard on the vehicle; it will pull sediment up into the filters and into the carburetor or fuel injection. And two, it's really thoughtless if someone else has to drive behind you and they have to fill the tank for you." My Dad always said that and so I always taught that to my children. That Friday, I broke my own rule: I drove home on almost empty, and thought "even if I have to, I'll run and get gas in it for whoever drives next." In other words, I rationalized.

Saturday morning came and my wife was up super early. She said, "I've got to take Amanda to go do her ACT test." We lived in a small town in Ohio, and she had to drive about 45 minutes to get to the testing site, so she had to leave at five in the morning. She took off and soon after I was getting ready to jump in the truck to get to work on all my planned projects, when she came driving back in the van. She said, "I need the keys to your truck." And I said "You can't have the keys to my truck. I'm going to use it." And she said "John, you left the van on empty. The nearest gas station isn't open yet. I need the keys to the truck." Well, I said "Fine." And I gave her the keys to my truck and then she drove away in my truck on Saturday morning destroying my plans for the day.

I fussed to myself, not to anybody else, just myself. I was planning to use that truck, and I kept trying to make up some sort of story that would make it not my fault and make it her fault. I'm pretty imaginative so I probably came fairly close, but I had to admit early on, "You know, you idiot, you're doing exactly what you teach other people not to do. One, you broke your own rule. Two, you're trying to make up a story that makes it someone else's fault and you're purposely distorting your own reality."

I felt terrible about that and by the time my wife got home I had dinner ready for her and the house was clean; I had to do some penance for my bad thoughts. The funny thing is, she never knew I had those thoughts. (Note to self: it's always best to repent before the thought turns into a deed.) That is an example of what can happen if we allow ourselves, sometimes purposefully, to become stuck in our own reality. This is where pride will take us, whereas, when I was humble, I came closer to the truth of the situation, which was simply that I had caused my own problem. What would my relationship with my wife have been like that evening if she had returned home and I had still been sullen and resentful, even if she had been responsible for the situation? But because I was able to turn from my pride and approach a situation with humility, not just once but many times throughout our marriage, (but mostly because my wife is a wonderful person) we have a strong and regenerative relationship today.

When I begin a coaching relationship, the client sometimes asks me, "What are the things that will help me to succeed as you're coaching, and what are the things that will get in the way of me being successful as I receive coaching?" I tell them that one of the most important things is, are you willing to listen to a perspective other than your own? Is pride going to stop you? Are you going to have walls of defense up because you want to look good rather than get better? There's a difference. Ironically, the need to be smart and have the right answers will stop you from gaining intelligence and getting the right answers. The need to blame and point fingers will be a barrier, because that will cause defensiveness in yourself and others.

Other values are equally capable of being based in principle or in counterfeit principles. The ones I have listed in the chart are by no means an exhaustive list, but they are ones that easily, and hopefully clearly, illustrate how our character traits lead us to the principles or the counterfeits.

Choice: Collaboration vs. Manipulation

Most people also value having choices. It is important to recognize that people use their agency to choose between different options, often using criteria that are different from ours. When we approach the value of choice from a principled standpoint, a standpoint that recognizes the agency of ourselves and others, we are eager to collaborate, to understand and to teach, to positively influence those around us so that, together, we can come to the best solution for a situation. In Stephen Covey's "Seven Habits of Highly Effective People,' Habit #4 is "Seek first to understand, then to be understood." When we are truly collaborative in our approach to someone's power of choice, when we recognize their agency, we will seek to understand them and the choices they make. We can then share our own viewpoints and knowledge in the hopes of helping them understand our choices and, yes, influencing theirs.

However, it is crucial to understand that all we can do is hope to influence, not control. Without that understanding and respect, our efforts will quickly turn to manipulation. Remember the story of the man in the Arbinger Institute's book "Leadership and Self Deception?" The one who felt he was being "smoothed?" This is why character matters: it colors our intentions and even if our outward behaviors don't noticeably change, people will still recognize the difference, if not immediately, then over time. Again, I'll paraphrase Stephen Covey: sometimes, no deal is the best deal. If getting what you want requires acting in bad character, in the long run, it's a lose-lose. If the only way you can get what you want is to manipulate and try to control others, you probably want the wrong thing and what you get won't be regenerative.

Sometimes, in fact quite often, people will choose things we do not want them to choose. Part of valuing choice from a principled perspective is recognizing and accepting the consequences of our and others' choices. If members of an organization cannot come to a collaborative decision, or can't get on board with executive decisions, no deal might be the only solution that respects everyone's agency. This can look like moving to another team, being taken off a certain assignment or given new duties. It might even look like an employee leaving the organization, voluntarily or otherwise. This is why a vision and mission as shown in our tree model, with true employee buy-in, that people choose to follow and want to achieve, are essential. It is why choosing employees and team members with positive character traits, leaders who set the right example and foster the right culture, and constantly returning to the Principles are very important.

Work Ethic: Focused, Sustained Effort vs. Rationalization

It's not hard to see why having a good work ethic would be valued by many organizations. Employers not only want, but need, employees willing to put in work to get results, to accomplish the mission, and employees value knowing that their hard work is appreciated, meaningful, and, yes, rewarded. The value is work ethic, and people who understand the principle of work and accomplishment, the law of the harvest, will put in focused, sustained effort to achieve their goals, whether personal or professional. People with a principled view of work and accomplishment will hate busywork, work for appearance's sake, and dog-and-pony shows. They want their work to mean something, to lead to valuable results.

In contrast, the negative character trait associated with work ethic is rationalization. There's an old saying: people often act as though results equals no results, plus a good story. They meant to get to that assignment, that chore, but... cue the good story, the explanation why accomplishing that task was impossible and they are in no way to blame for this outcome. This is something I run into frequently in my line of work: people who are good at managing (or manipulating) relationships and the narrative to absolve themselves of guilt when work is not accomplished. Often others don't realize that this is what is happening in the moment, but over time you will see a consistent pattern of poor performance or low accomplishment, of work that didn't get done in time or at all.

Rebekah: Sometimes, the people who are gifted at rationalizing, or at being constantly overwhelmed, don't realize what they are doing or how to stop. I worked with a fellow Staff Sergeant in the Marine Corps who was constantly overwhelmed. To be fair, he didn't have an easy job; it involved managing almost 30 Marines around the clock on a guard duty. Something was always going wrong: someone was sick and couldn't cover their shift, an inspection was coming up and they weren't prepared, a personal problem would surprise him and interfere with work. We worked in the same building and had the same 1st Sergeant (or supervisor) and I heard perhaps more than I really wanted to about the issue from both of them. But this fellow Staff Sergeant epitomized the saying: results equal no results, plus a good story.

He always had an apology, an excuse, a reason why he was late to a meeting, late to formation, why his Marines hadn't received their shots or qualified on the rifle range or for the physical fitness test. I felt bad for him because he seemed to be a nice man who was genuinely in over his head. One day he had arrived late for a meeting, almost missing it entirely, and as soon as he walked in the door, he had an apology and a story already pouring out. 1st Sergeant just held up his hand and said "I told you before, don't apologize and don't explain. Sit down." He then finished the meeting without another word to the Staff Sergeant.

I honestly believe he did not get the training and support he needed from his leaders, so he fell back on what he had: rationalization. In the Marine Corps, it's hard to fire people. You can move them around, although a shortage of manpower sometimes makes that difficult, and this Staff Sergeant was eventually reassigned to a position with less responsibility. I sometimes wonder how that worked out, if he found a place where he fit better, with better leadership, or was he still constantly overwhelmed? But in the civilian world, you can fire people who aren't performing. It comes at a cost to the organization and that is where good leadership comes in, but if the cost of keeping someone is greater than the cost of replacing them, the logical step is clear. Work Ethic can't just be aspirational, it has to be motivational and lead to Accomplishment.

Relationships: Sacrifice vs. Selfishness

It is common for people and organizations to say they value relationships. Individually and collectively, an organizational culture's dominant character traits will make a big difference in how relationships are developed and even defined. A person who is in the habit of putting themselves first, of viewing the world in terms of how it affects them, (someone who is ego-centric) will view relationship through that lens as well: how does this relationship benefit or affect me? Am I getting what I want? Am I being fulfilled? There is no clear or meaningful effort to build mutually beneficial relationships, or to pursue win-win solutions if a win-lose will do. Even without active malice or consciously nefarious strategies, selfishness can only lead to exploitation, and exploitation will drain your organization of its best members and potential, requiring a constant infusion of outside resources to keep it alive.

Sacrifice is a word that is easy to misunderstand. In both the business world and society at large. I've heard folks recoil from the concept of sacrifice. "Why can't I have it all? I shouldn't have to give up anything." The best and most concise definition I've heard is that sacrifice is giving up something good for something better. In this understanding your mission is imperative. How will you know the difference between good, better, and best if you don't know what your mission is? The correct definition of mission provides a sound foundation for love. Remember, mission is knowing who your stakeholders are and what they need from you. Mission is knowing who you serve. There is no greater example of love exemplified in sacrifice than that of the Savior of the world. "Greater love has no man than this, that a man lay down his life for his friends." John 15:13. Christ, more than any other, understood his mission and knew what it would take to contribute to the success of others.

Though we are very unlikely to be called to that level of sacrifice, we do have daily opportunities to practice this character trait. Am I willing to sacrifice sleep to tend to a crying child so my wife can get some rest?

Am I willing to sacrifice some of my share of the budget so another department can accomplish a goal critical to the company's mission? Am I willing to sacrifice my ego for the value of learning?

An example of selfishness? Look back at the story of me bringing the car home almost empty... Not proud of that one.

As with all character traits, we are not limited to two extremes. Think instead in terms of a spectrum. In between are traits like civility, respect, forgiveness, empathy, etc.

Innovation: Abundance Mentality vs. Predation or Parasitic

As my friend mentioned, innovation as a value was very important at his company, as it is in other organizations. Imagine the innovations that have defined our age: the computer, internet, and mobile communication. And how many innovations, how many variations have sprung from those inventions? What if, instead of imagining how to improve on and develop the computer, early innovators thought "Oh no, someone got ahead of me. How can I take his invention, how can I take his market share? How can I squash this computer thing and keep people dependent on pencils and paper?" Instead, they thought, "What an amazing thing! How can I make it better? How can I add value for myself and others?" That is an abundance mentality. It is necessary in every aspect of our lives, from business to ministering to politics. Without an abundance mentality, our focus turns inward; instead of asking "How can I add value?" we ask "How can I benefit? How can I get my share of this?" We become predatory or even parasitic. We act out of fear instead of hope or faith, we become defensive instead of progressive.

When we are acting out of fear, out of a "there's only so much pie to go around" mindset, our focus shifts. We no longer think, "How can I progress, how can I move forward, what are the possibilities?" Instead we think, "How can I hold others back? How can I keep *them* from getting ahead of *me*?" I learned this lesson in elementary school track. I was a relatively fast runner in grade school. When I got to high school it turns out I wasn't that fast, I was never a great athlete, but in my small pond, I was a pretty good athlete until my pond got bigger. I was probably the fastest kid in my grade school, and yet I was losing all my races. My Uncle Billy came to one of my track meets once. After the meet he said "John, when you're running, watch the finish line. Don't watch the other runners." I was so worried about getting beat that I kept looking at the other runners. And so, someone was always ahead of me, it's easier to watch others when they're ahead of you! I said, "Ok Uncle Billy," and I followed his advice. I started watching the finish line and trying to get there just as fast as I possibly could without worrying about the other runners. I could feel them on my heels, and that probably helped, but I was watching the finish line. And amazingly, at that age, I started winning a lot more races.

Even though I never became a track star, the lesson has always been of great value. What's your goal? What are you trying to accomplish? So, in business, it's just ingrained in me not to worry about the competition. What's the best I can do? What's the most creative I can be? If other people succeed, I'm going to be happy for them too. If they succeed ahead of me, that's fine because I'll probably learn something. It's just a brighter world. And yet, I don't know how many people I've met over the years who are very proud of their predatory or parasitic method of accomplishment: beat the competition, crush them. What's your goal really? Do you really go into business to beat someone? Or do you go into business to create something, to serve others? Some do because that's how they were taught to compete in their early years and that's the kind of grownup they became. I don't want to work or live in that culture. I recently conducted a strategic planning retreat for a client. A guest speaker shared research showing that 60% of value is lost when leaders over-focus on the competition.

Dwight, a CEO friend of ours shared this experience: Innovation is what keeps you moving forward successfully in challenging times. At the beginning of the Covid 19 pandemic of 2020, which saw many businesses struggling to survive, one former client (and current friend) decided not to wait around to let that happen to his computer systems company. When it became apparent that many communities (even whole countries) were going to be locked down, he met with his leadership team and decided they needed to get ahead of the curve and start moving everyone to remote work. They met on a Monday, decided to go remote on a Tuesday, and by Friday, everybody was working off-site and remote. Their next step was to come up with a plan to help their clients quickly transition from in-office to remote work as well. They decided what to do and how to get everything set up so their clients' employees could work safely and securely from home, even before their first client called asking for help going remote. They took about 40 organizations from working on site to working remote inside of two weeks.

The CEO said of that time, "Our clients are calling me saying, 'Your team showed up on Monday, by Wednesday morning, I had 45 people working remote. Everybody was able to dial in, it was secure. So, our hit on productivity wasn't 3 or 4 weeks, it was 24 hours, and we were back in business.' And our team did that. Pretty great, right? We're very appreciative of their efforts. That was something that wasn't anticipated. We had to stabilize our environments, technology wise, and then stabilize each and every one of our clients so that they were able to continue to run their business."

That's innovation and abundance mentality. They didn't sit around bemoaning their fate and what was happening to *them*. They didn't have a scarcity mentality; they didn't start thinking "How can we beat the competition or take their market share?" They asked "How can we bring value to our clients in this time? How can we help them fulfill their missions?" The character trait of abundance mentality allowed their value of innovation to become regenerative by tapping into the principle of creation.

Again, these positive, regenerative character traits work in concert with other positive character traits. If you are humble, you are also more likely to be collaborative because you recognize the value of others' perspectives and contributions. When you have an abundance mentality, you recognize the value of work and are willing to put in sustained, focused effort to create value, to create your vision for the future. Negative, depleting traits attract and engender other negative traits. When we approach honesty from a place of pride, we are also less likely to recognize the inherent value of others, especially if their realities differ from or challenge our own. This narrow perspective can lead to selfishness, manipulation to get others to see things our way. The other day I heard someone say, "I've never learned anything from someone I agree with."

Why Character Matters

People who say, "I'm just being honest," or who pride themselves on calling it like it is, are only calling it the way *they* see it, only recognize the realities that fit their viewpoint or narrative, that will lead to the outcome they want. Many people who pride themselves on being honest at all costs, on telling it like it is, are often approaching honesty from a position of pride. You can be honest and a jerk, and the irony is that in this situation, your honesty comes from an incomplete or distorted perspective because you are only acknowledging or aware of a portion of the truth, rather than the whole. Or, as my mom would say: "Only fools are positive." As I mentioned in the experience with my oldest daughter, beware of false dichotomies. There will never be a time when you have to sacrifice one value for the sake of another if your values are principle-based and you are promoting and acquiring regenerative, positive character traits. You will never have to sacrifice honesty for respect, or choice for an abundance mentality. Sometimes, when a win-win situation is not possible, the best choice is to walk away. But decisions like these ensure you are living up to and preserving your values, rather than sacrificing them for short term gains.

You may have heard the expression "Character is destiny," our character is a result of our choices made every day, day after day. It is not an accident of birth or completely attributable to upbringing. We can choose to correct bad habits, turn away from false teachings. And we can choose to be rooted in the rich, fertile soil of sound principle.

These are all spectrums. No one has perfect character all the time. There are times when I act prideful, there are times when I act selfishly, but is that who I am or is that a moment? If I allow that to continue, it becomes who I am, and I wouldn't know it because my thinking gets skewed, my categories get hardened. But if I am rooted in principle, if I take time to assess myself and my actions, I can make corrections as I go. I can recognize that I acted selfishly and apologize. I can see that I'm not respecting someone else's agency and try to engage with them in a more respectful, collaborative way. Then my character will improve, my values will be rooted in principles, and I will progress. My organization will progress and grow and the values, my roots, will grow deeper and deeper. There is no such thing as having too strong of values, or too good a character. I will never be too humble, have too strong a work ethic, have too much of an abundancy mentality. I will never be too honest. I might be disrespectful, but that's a love problem, not an honesty problem. When I develop my compassion, my sense of sacrifice and respect for others, I can never be too honest because I would never confuse honesty with rudeness. Positive character traits root our values, our organizations, in principles.

Years ago, I worked with people with cognitive disabilities, what at the time was defined as mental retardation. For a bit of perspective, I'm 6'4", I've always been strong, so I often was one of the team members who worked with people given to violent outbursts, with the assumption that I would be the one to control them when they 'acted out.' However, that's not in my nature and not what I wanted to do. So, I learned from John McGee, author of Gentle Teaching and through a great deal of study and practicing different sets of skills, how to not physically control people who were having violent outbursts. I became very skilled at dealing with aggressive residents, at keeping myself safe while deescalating frightening or violent situations. As a matter of fact, I became the expert at it in my company, and I was given the opportunity to teach our associates and other organizations how to create healthy relationships with people in their care, how to influence without controlling them physically.

During this time, I worked at a children's home, and one of the departments in the home was the respite department. When parents or caregivers needed a break or time for a date or night out, they would bring their child or even grown children to this department of the children's home because no one else could meet their needs. One couple would do this with their adult son. He was about my height and at least 70 pounds heavier, a very big young man. I was asked to come work with this young man because the last time he was there, he broke a woman's arm, he grabbed her hand and twisted until it fractured and dislocated her shoulder. He also broke another person's ribs and put her through a big plate glass window.

So, they called me in to work with this young man the next time he came in and I thought, yeah, sure, I want to work with this guy. I spent time with him for a while and used all my skills to keep him calm, to get him to trust me so that he wouldn't lose control and become violent. That worked for a while, but as you've probably guessed, eventually, he had an outburst. He was very big and very strong, probably stronger than me. I had all the self-defense skills and holds necessary to protect myself, I had been very well trained, but I wasn't just trying to stay safe, I was trying to earn his trust. I was trying to get him to not be so afraid, to feel safe and comfortable so that he wouldn't have an outburst. I used every skill I could think of, and I was considered very skilled. And yet, nothing. It just got worse and worse. He seemed to be relentless.

Finally, this violent, out of control man threw himself on the floor in a position I recognized: spreadeagle, arms out, still for just a moment. I knew what had just happened: he expected me to perform a "takedown." When a person with severe behavior problems can't or won't control their own behavior, that duty falls on the caregiver; it becomes their job to control that person. It's sort of an emotional welfare: "I can't handle the responsibility, you do it for me." Earlier that week, this young man had a similar outburst and seven caregivers were required to hold him in that position until he was "calm."

As I saw him, spread out on the floor, emotionally exhausted, I realized I had been seeing him as this very frightening, very big man, like a warrior or adversary. At that time, my youngest child was four, and he would throw tantrums like any four-year-old. And when he was exhausted, physically and emotionally, he would throw himself on the floor. In that moment, I recognized what was happening with this young man. I thought: "Wait, he's having a tantrum, he's acting like my son, it's just that he's not four years old." And as soon as I saw him as a scared human being instead of my adversary or opponent, in that moment, he started calming down.

I don't remember doing anything differently, but he started reaching out to me to hold my hand for a few moments before he pulled away, instead of trying to break my hand. Before, he'd reach out to grab and want to twist, to break, anything to hurt me, to get me to back off. I was using all the skills that should have taught him to trust me and they didn't work. As soon as I saw him differently, all those skills magically started kicking in. It wasn't an instant transformation, but by the end of the afternoon we had walked to the gym, played basketball, we sat together and did puzzles. And when his parents came, he didn't want to leave. They were in absolute shock, because every other time, when his parents came, he ran for the car. Every time he came back, he and I were friends and we just hung out. I didn't have to manage his behavior.

Now it's important to remember that I did need all that training, all those skills I had acquired to protect myself and earn his trust; just having good intentions would not have solved this problem. But there are several lessons here. One is the lesson of character; how do you see people? Another is the lesson of knowing the difference between trying to manage someone and trying to lead them. You can't lead someone unless you see the good in them. If you can't see the good, you won't be able to influence them, not in a positive way. All of my skills weren't enough to help lead and influence this young man until they were backed up by a change in my viewpoint, in my character. As an executive coach, I recognize this as a paradigm shift, as a father and a Christian I recognize the power of a change of heart.

Of all the things I've taught over the years, a lot of it goes back to that moment. As humans, we vary greatly in our God-given abilities as well as the effort and discipline we put into developing them. But emotionally, we're not that different. That's the point. We all experience fear. If we act out of fear rather than faith, our influence will be significantly limited. If we act out of scarcity rather than abundance, selfishness rather than sacrifice, our influence and our outcomes will be negative. My character was flawed as long as I saw him in a negative light. As soon as I could see him with compassion, rooted in the principles of love and truth, my character improved and I became more worthy of his trust. I couldn't manage his trust, but I could earn it, I could influence it. All the skills in the world will not make up for poor character.

Jon, another client and friend, said to us: "You have to know the principles; you have to live the principles. Because a lot of people know them but not as many people live by them. Character is everything. I saw this statement 30 years ago: it takes a lifetime to build your character, it takes seconds to lose it. With my female employees, they know they'll never get a cheap look from me, ever, it won't happen. That's a learned behavior. If someone sees you out of character, you're done. Once you begin to slip, it's almost impossible to get back to a good place."

As Jon said, building character takes time and effort, and consistently trying to do the right thing. It doesn't mean you have to be perfect: we're all human and make mistakes and most people will accept that (when accompanied by a sincere apology and efforts to right wrongs). But continuous inconsistencies and hypocrisies will be noticed and destroy trust and relationships. Leaders with poor character will destroy relationships and derail an organization.

CHAPTER 5

PRACTICES

PLAN

MISSION

VISION

VALUES

PRINCIPLES

VISION

If we continue following our tree analogy, from the roots or values should come a vision. I want to take a moment to distinguish having a Vision from having vision. Both are important to your success as an individual or an organization.

Having vision

Having vision is objective in nature. This is connected to the principle of Truth. What makes vision regenerative is doing the work required to align it with truth. The question is: does my vision draw from sound principle or am I rooted in counterfeits? Can you see things as they really are or is your reality skewed?

Having vision is accomplished by taking a realistic look at the factors that will impact your success. Those factors can include: the political environment you are working in; how the ecological environment will affect your business or how your business will affect the ecology; the impact or demands of regulatory compliance; having the right team in place to succeed; being aware of economic factors like competitors, stock markets, market share, etc.; the overall impact of the social climate on your business and the impact your business may have on the social climate; the technology available and required for you to efficiently accomplish your mission.

In other words, are you willing and able to do the due diligence required to understand your impact and opportunities given the circumstances of the world you exist in?

Having a Vision

Where there is no vision, the people perish: but he that keepeth the law, happy is he. Proverbs 29:18

Having a Vision is largely subjective, it is about creating a clear picture of what you are shooting for. We define it as "The desired reality to come." What will success look like? What do you want to be or become as an individual or an organization? Examples: "I would like to be wise and kind". Or "Our Company will be a place where people enjoy their work and others value the work we do." Having a vision is the thing that causes us to get up and get moving, to overcome inertia. Often it is what helps us to overcome fear, fear of failure, fear of success, fear of the unknown.

When narrowing down on what your vision for your company is, here are a few questions to ask to see if it will pass the test:

- Do you find this vision compelling and easy to grasp?
- Does it connect with the stated values?
- Does it clearly distinguish the future from the present?
- Will it be exciting and understandable to a broad base of people in the organization?
- Do you believe the organization can realize the vision if leadership and management is fully committed to it?

Remember, while your plans and practices should be adapted on a regular basis, your vision should provide a point of focus to help people know what they are aiming for. Your values and vision will attract people who want to align with and support them and will find meaning in the work your organization does. Changing your vision or not living up to it will come across as hypocritical and inconsistent and drive away the stakeholders you need to make your vision a reality. As our friend Jon said, "Vision doesn't really change. I think if a company is constantly changing their vision, they really lack direction."

Visions don't have to be complicated. In fact, the most compelling vision is often very simple. If you ask Beth of consulting company Change 4 Growth, what her company stands for, she will tell you "It's helping people. At the end of the day, it's so many different types of helping... really helping organizations and individuals reach their highest potentials." The only caveats we can think of when it comes to vision being permanent would be 1. Your vision should grow and expand over time. An example may be going from being a startup company to continued growth or sustaining success. In this case, it's not so much that your vision changes. Rather, it's very much like the main trunk of our tree. Over time, the vision grows into what's next. Just like the rings on a tree that occur as the tree grows year after year. Or 2. When you progress on your journey and discover it's not really where you want to go. This is an opportunity to revisit your values and build a vision based on what you've learned. Sometimes you can find the road you want to be on as a contrast to the road you don't want to be on.

Have you really taken the time to evaluate your vision? Is it really what you or your organization are about? Does everyone know and understand it? If not, then you might need to rethink your stated vision or rethink how you share it. If, and this is a big if, you realize that your stated vision isn't your true objective, then you will need to go back to the beginning and find your why: what will success look like? Why do you do what you do? What is your desired reality? And then be very transparent in communicating this to your stakeholders: own your mistake or misunderstanding, own the changes you need to make, and very openly communicate every step of the way.

Rebekah: When I left the Marine Corps, while I was still not sure what my next steps would be, I began volunteering to help Syrian refugees in Columbus, Ohio. We offered English tutoring for women and homework help for students in the evenings. For a while I thought about pursuing a career working with refugees. At the time I was doing administrative work for Dad and was beginning to see and understand the kind of impact his work had on his clients, their companies, and even their families. It took a couple of years, but I eventually realized it was a work I wanted to be a part of too. From the outside, that might seem like a bit of a leap: going from working with refugees to leadership coaching. I felt that way myself for a time. But when I finally narrowed down on what my personal vision for my life is, it made more sense. I want to help people to make their lives better. When you look at my education and career choices from that perspective, it doesn't seem so inconsistent after all. Tutoring refugees, I was trying to help them create a better life for themselves in a new country, new language, new culture. Through leadership coaching, I can help teach people the principles, character traits, and skills for them to be more successful in their roles, to benefit their career, organization, and even personal life. We try to help people learn to be the best, happiest versions of themselves, to be the leaders they always wanted to be. Even joining the Marine Corps was about wanting to help people, people in my own country and people in bad situations in other countries. To get the truest form of buy-in, people need to be able to align their personal vision for themselves with the vision for the organizations they're a part of.

No one can align to a vision that is unclear or poorly communicated. Being a leader means not only having a clear vision, but being able to share it in a way that others can see it, can get excited about wanting to create it. Your vision is your purpose. Next, you have to be able to make it a reality.

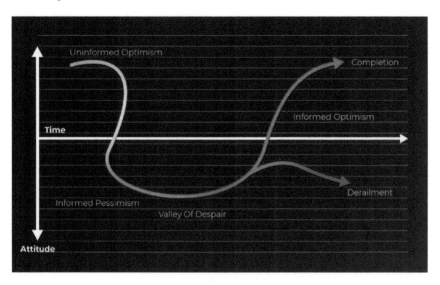

Adapted from: Emotional Cycles of Change, Dan Kelly and Daryl Conner.
The Annual Handbook for Group Facilitators 1979

The work of fine art above helps to see the importance of having a vision. A CEO asked how to stay motivated and help associates to stay motivated through the normal challenges that come with growth and change (call them growing pains). First point: "Where there is no vision, the people perish..." We generally start out on our journey of change with optimism and positive energy (uniformed optimism). Soon after, we run into inevitable challenges. We go through the realization of the difficulties and struggles that come with change or transition (informed pessimism). Without a vision of where we are going, we can't see how the 'valley of despair' is worth the struggle. Feeling lost in the valley without a vision of the big picture, we become disoriented. This can lead to derailment.

It's the job and responsibility of the leader to help people to be oriented within the overall journey. Being in the valley is tough but it's worth it. Second point: "...He who keepeth the law, happy is he." The leader's role is to help people stay the course. This is not so much about creating certainty as it is about navigating through uncertainty and making it through to accomplish the goal everyone was excited about in the first place.

CHAPTER 6

PRACTICES

PLAN

MISSION

VISION

VALUES

PRINCIPLES

MISSION

If a vision is your or your organization's big picture goal, the desired reality to come, a Mission is your basis for making the vision a reality: it is an explanation of how that shared purpose will serve all of your stakeholders. When we talk about strategy, we start with the mission. Mission is the transition from aspiration to execution.

Does your Mission pass the test?

- Does it align with your stated values and vision?
- Is this purpose inspiring to you?
- Do you think it would be valid 30 years from now and could extend beyond your current products, markets and channels?
- Does this purpose help you decide what not to pursue as well as what to pursue?
- Is this purpose authentic and does it clearly articulate what business you are in?
- Do you think this purpose would be greeted with enthusiasm throughout the organization?
- How will this purpose benefit each stakeholder?

Taking a look at our organizational tree model again, the Vision is the trunk: it draws power from the soil, through roots and then feeds the mission which provides the basis for the plans. The vision is what holds it all together. The Mission is where you start to identify the key stakeholders of your organization. Once you've identified who they are and how you will serve them, your plans and practices will be built based on your mission statement.

The importance of a Mission Statement

A mission statement is not a few magic words that inspire the otherwise confused masses to greatness. Nor is it orders from the boss to tell employees what's really important around here.

No, there is nothing intrinsically magical about a mission statement. A mission statement in which employees have no ownership or put no value is more likely to motivate negatively than positively. One of the major benefits of mission statements also happens to be what creates great risk. A mission statement serves to help judge the integrity of actions and decisions with the stated values of the company. Therefore, if actions or decisions are consistently considered to not be in line with stated values, the integrity of the actor(s) or decision maker(s) is suspect, maybe even ridiculed. After all, nobody likes a hypocrite.

Though no one intends to act in ways that encourage others to label them harshly, negative conclusions do commonly occur when others can't see the connection between what is said and what is done. It's that if-I-don't-know-I'll-make-it-up thing. When we do make it up, for some reason it's seldom pretty. In other words, if we're not walking the talk, what we say will come back to hurt us.

Understanding even some of the risk, why would anyone ever want to invest time and money in developing a mission statement?

A mission statement reflects a deep understanding of mutual purpose, giving all actions taken on behalf of the company united value and direction. It can serve as a gauge – even a lodestar – by which the value of actions and decisions can be measured. To each individual, a mission statement can provide a sense of personal direction and orientation within the company. "I get the big picture and know how I can contribute."

All work and initiatives should feed back into the mission statement: employees should clearly see that line and alignment.

According to Stephen Covey, trust is the highest form of human motivation. Though most of us readily acknowledge the value of a high-trust environment, we often feel the negative results of violated trust and don't even know how we got there. For many of us, trust is either there or it isn't. What value, then, would we put on being able to deliberately create the conditions of trust?

The ability to identify or create mutual purpose is essential in establishing conditions of trust. If I know that you want what I want, I don't have to worry about manipulation or hidden agendas. A mission statement that is well conceived, written, communicated and integrated into the company's culture can provide the basis of trust to help an organization move forward. Of course, that's only the beginning. Good leadership and management require using this focal point to measure the worth of ongoing behaviors and doing so in a way that is motivating and logical.

Creating a Mission Statement

An effective mission statement considers all of the stakeholders of the company. Stakeholders usually include employees, customers or clients, shareholders or investors, vendors, and community, among others depending on the situation or industry. How will your organization's vision become a reality for each of your stakeholders? What will it look like for them? Will customers receive high quality products and service? Will employees feel valued and fulfilled in doing meaningful work?

The mission statement helps assess and balance the needs of all of the stakeholders. If we truly believe "the customer is always right," we may soon find we are unable to meet customer demands. Without the commitment of investors, employees, vendors, and the community, we will find the resources required to meet our obligations are lacking or not there at all. Likewise, focusing only on any one of the stakeholders and/ or neglecting any of the other stakeholders exposes an Achilles heel. This vulnerability can often prove to be an unexpected setback or downfall just when we're moving full speed ahead and we think the world is our oyster. With this in mind, a balanced mission can create a solid foundation upon which lasting success can be built. Having clearly identified and articulated the needs of each stakeholder group provides the basis for a relevant strategic plan. This same sense of mission will allow the organization to measure the success of that plan.

In the development of a mission statement, process is more important than product. Experience has taught that involvement is a major factor in commitment. If you want employees to be committed to the interests of the company, they need to be significantly involved in the process. "I am more willing to commit to 'our' cause than 'your' cause." Level of commitment is a far better predictor of success than brilliance of strategy. While it might not be practical to gather all stakeholders in a room and dialogue a mission statement, sharing the mission statement draft and inviting and *acting on* feedback is a great place to start and invite involvement.

In the final analysis, it comes down to what we want and what we're willing to do about it. Developing a mission statement isn't a quick and easy process; not if we want to do it right. If done poorly or we're not willing to commit to it, it may even do more harm than good. And yet, if we want to be a great company and not just good, the process of developing a mission statement can be an essential contribution to a company of qualified, committed people working together to accomplish mutual purpose.

Rebekah: My last two years in the Marine Corps, I was the Substance Abuse Control officer for our battalion of about 500 Marines. The mission role of this position was to help ensure the safety and wellbeing of the Marines in my Command. The practical, less glamorous aspect of this position meant that I was in charge of training the Marines on the dangers of drug and alcohol abuse, setting up counseling and treatment for Marines with qualified counselors, and conducting regular drug and alcohol testing at the battalion. So, at the daily level, I called up Marines and told them to come pee in a cup. I then packaged and labeled that little sample bottle and sent it off to be tested. As you can imagine, latex gloves and sanitizer played a big role in my day to day life! Here's why this story is relevant: I did not wake up every day excited about dealing with urine. My position wasn't exciting, certainly not the Call of Duty action many think of when you mention the Marines. But my work was bearable and even meaningful because I absolutely supported my battalion's mission and saw my role in it. No one wants to be deployed to a combat zone with someone who is going through withdrawal from untreated substance issues, or training on a rifle range next to a Marine who is high, or even driving around base next to a drunk driver. If I focused on just my daily job, it was boring and even gross. But by understanding my part in supporting our mission, a mission I was aligned with, my job was meaningful and worthwhile.

Once you have your mission statement and buy in from your stake-holders, you're ready to put that mission into action. Strategy, by our definition, begins with a mission. Principles, Values, and Vision are required to set the stage for a sound strategic plan. They help you identify and articulate your aspirations. Strategy begins when you identify who you serve and what you provide. Strategy is creating your plan to meet the needs of each of these 'stakeholders.' Your next step is to create and evaluate your plans and practices with this question in mind: How does this serve our stakeholders? How does this align with our mission?

It is not uncommon for leaders to create a mission statement and not experience any impact or benefit in creating the culture and outcomes they want. This is often because a mission is thought of as a marketing tool. A mission is not the same as your brand. The entire tree creates the anatomy of your culture. Your brand is what your culture looks like from the outside.

In one case, we were working with an executive team to develop their strategic plan. When we told them of the importance of this model, they were skeptical. They had gone through the process of creating a mission at least three times before. They said they had seen no benefit to the day-to-day operation of their business.

It was gratifying to see the lights go on when they went through this process. They could see the pertinence of having a mission that provides a foundation for decision making and discretionary effort. They even found, in addition to being a resource for effective leadership, living their mission provided the opportunity to create a brand that rang true. Their brand ended up being a genuine expression of their culture.

CHAPTER 7

PRACTICES

PLAN

MISSION

VISION

VALUES

PRINCIPLES

PLANS

The process of developing a business strategy includes creating a plan on how you'll keep the promises your mission makes to each of your stakeholders.

Vickey was tasked with turning around a struggling community college. She had both vision and a vision, and a very clear mission to fulfill. When asked how she went about carrying out her difficult job and revitalizing a struggling organization, she said "Everything we do has to lead us toward our mission." She started with building a team with shared values: not a team with exactly the same skills and outlook, but that valued what she was trying to accomplish. They shared her vision of where they wanted the organization to go, how it would grow. She added, "We live and breathe mission, vision and values and purpose. What is our purpose to this community? What do we do for our students? And how do we help them get to where they want to go? We live it every day."

As Vicky said, everything has to lead you toward your mission, how you are fulfilling your promise to your stakeholders. Every policy, practice, process, should be aligned with your values and vision and should lead back to that line in your mission statement about how you will make your vision a reality for this stakeholder.

For our purposes, we'll focus on plans and practices that help us build a culture of trust and integrity. Primarily this applies to working with those for whom we have stewardship as a leader. We have found this approach can be effective with all our stakeholders.

Discussing the Undiscussable

Early in my coaching career the CEO of a construction company asked me to work with a leader I'll call Bob. For many reasons Bob was highly valued and highly regarded by many of his stakeholders, specifically upper management, and customers. He was described as hard-working and dedicated. He was very intelligent and regarded as a problem-solver committed to getting results.

Then came the weaknesses or areas that caused concern: Bob wasn't as highly regarded by the people who reported to him. In short, they were terrified by him. It turned out, he was about six foot six inches tall, weighing in at over 250 pounds of solid muscle. He had played college and semi-pro football and was a relatively young man who had lost none of his strength.

Bob had been known for his violent outbursts, including kicking out the door of the office trailer and throwing a full four-drawer filing cabinet. This being the case, I chose for our first meeting to be a lunch meeting at a restaurant.

When we met, we began getting to know each other by talking about family and personal interests. Bob's description of his relationship with his wife and children was tender and loving. He talked of a close friendship with his wife and how much he enjoyed being with his children and coaching their sports teams.

We then talked about his professional relationships. As we talked about the situations described above, Bob didn't seem overly concerned about them causing any real problems. I asked if he had any similar outbursts at home with his family. Bob seemed to be appalled at the thought of such a thing. 'He would never treat his family that way.' He couldn't believe I would even suggest such a thing.

I asked how he had such good self-control at home but lost his temper so spectacularly at work. He smiled tolerantly at me and explained: "You don't understand, I never lose my temper." (*If you're a bit confused at this moment, just think how I felt.*) He went on to say: "That's just good theatre. I am responsible for a multi-million-dollar project. When the customer has a concern or a complaint, I make sure he knows I take it seriously and will get results. He knows I'll do whatever it takes to solve the problem.

He couldn't see either the ethical cost of how he treated employees or the business cost to motivation, commitment, and engagement. He just knew, he got results.

Now comes the moment of great peril and a pivotal learning opportunity for me. I said, "can you understand when I see that you have one set of values for how you treat your family and another set of values for how you treat your direct reports, I would question your integrity?" He almost came over the table at me! "Nobody questions my integrity! You need to understand, that is very important to me!"

I quickly explained I meant no disrespect. I helped him to understand when I'm talking about integrity and trust, I'm talking about structure. I wasn't judging his worth as a person. In the following conversation and throughout our working relationship, we worked on what you have already read throughout this book.

The lessons learned and the principles and practices that could come from this one conversation would fill another book. For our purposes, I want to focus on the leader's responsibility to build trust by creating a culture of organizational integrity. Bob was creating a degenerative culture that mined the energy and life out of people. The focus was on the fruit, not the soil.

Integrity and Trust

People usually avoid talking about integrity and trust because these words can cause people to become defensive. They think their character is being attacked. Questioning someone's integrity can feel like a personal assault. This becomes an insurmountable sticking point. If you can't talk about integrity and trust, you can't shape the culture you want. When you can see the anatomy of integrity and trust and their effect on outcome, you can begin to understand how to create culture by building integrity that results in trust.

If you were getting ready to get on a ship and cross the ocean, you would want to feel confident the ship could get you safely to your destination in a timely manner. Let's say you asked the captain, "Can you tell me a little more about this ship's integrity?"

If the captain comes back with a laundry list of nice things about that ship ("it was built in the USA," "it has air-conditioned cabins," or "drinks are always free") you will know almost nothing about that ship's ability to carry you safely across the ocean.

Instead, when we say a ship has integrity, we mean that it has the ability to set a course and stay on course. It has the ability to maintain a steady direction, hold up in a storm, and not come apart when the seas get rough. A ship with integrity can reliably stay the course, move at a reasonably steady rate, and arrive at its destination at a relatively predictable time.

Rebekah: For my last few years in the Marines, my direct supervisor was the Battalion Executive Officer (second in command of the battalion). I managed the battalion substance abuse and equal opportunity programs and reported directly to him about test results, trainings, inspections, etcetera. He used to call me a "fire-and-forget" weapon, meaning he only had to give me an order once and I would make it happen. He trusted me completely to accomplish the goals of our unit. He didn't trust me because I was nice, or smart, or honest. It wasn't because he liked the way I saluted or how neat I kept my office. We didn't share a faith, taste in music, or a birthday. He trusted me because I was aligned with the unit mission and I could accomplish my portion of that mission without handholding. A "fire-and-forget" weapon. And in return, I knew that I could tell him if I couldn't accomplish a task for whatever reason: if I needed additional resources, if there wasn't sufficient time, or if I needed to research a topic before I could even give him a time-frame for task completion. He could give me an order and trust I would follow it without excuses or dropping the ball, and I could trust that I would not be chastised or belittled for asking for support when I needed it.

Too often we fail to have meaningful conversations about trust because we assume it has to do with our value as a person. In most everyday conversations, we think of trust as a cosmic force that you either have or you don't. Few people are aware of our ability to build trust. As we can see in Rebekah's example, trust is not a personality trait or a value, but the result of personal and organizational integrity.

Failing to cultivate trust results in low empowerment; people talk about low trust in victim terminology (e.g., "I just can't trust him," "I don't know who to trust"). When people succeed, they tend to give the credit to how much they trust their team. When they fail, they tend to insist that low trust was the cause, without acknowledging their own stake in the interaction. There are always ways to influence any situation to promote the outcomes you want and minimize those you do not want, even if you do not have total control over the situation. Total control is impossible; influence is not only possible, it's inevitable. You are always influencing, whether you know it or not. I always say: Rule Number 1 of leadership is to know the difference between control and influence. The only person you have control of is yourself. With everyone else, all you have is influence. The objective as a leader is to have effective influence strategies.

Influencing the level of trust in your organization involves breaking it down into its components, assessing them, and then re-framing the ways you think and talk about trust on the individual and overall levels.

When trust is not cultivated, leaders find those they lead: don't know what's expected of them when directions are unclear or don't make sense; become resistant when motives are suspect; do only what is expected and no more; insist that "it's our policy" when creativity would be more helpful; or practice "malicious compliance" by doing exactly what they are told to do when they know the outcome will be bad. Cultivating trust in your organization creates a culture that is perfectly designed to accomplish your mission. You will be able to lead more than you manage because everyone performs at a higher level when you have organizational integrity.

Integrity is two things: alignment and engagement. In organizations, alignment looks like a shared set of values, visions, and mission. Engagement is drive and consists of capabilities and getting results: it's the principle of action and interaction requiring necessary skills and resources to accomplish tasks and produce outcomes. Both alignment and engagement are necessary for organizational integrity.

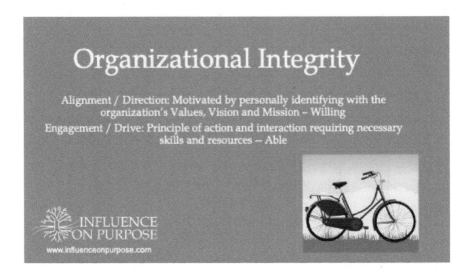

Organizational Integrity

Alignment / Direction: Motivated by personally identifying with the organization's Values, Vision and Mission – Willing
Engagement / Drive: Principle of action and interaction requiring necessary skills and resources – Able

INFLUENCE ON PURPOSE
www.influenceonpurpose.com

To simplify this idea even further, think about a bicycle. A bicycle is a good illustration because of two integrated functions: the rider is able to steer the bicycle and they are able to pedal it to a chosen destination.

The steering components of the bike represent alignment. When the front wheel is balanced and in good condition and the handlebars are secured and lined up with the wheel, you get on that bicycle, choose your direction and stay on course easily. That's alignment. But, if the chain is rusted and the back wheel is missing spokes and the tire is flat, the engagement will be very low. No matter how hard you point that bike in the right direction, you will struggle to pedal there without immense force. A bicycle with great alignment but bad engagement will struggle to move; it's useless.

In an organization, high alignment but low engagement looks like a group of people that talk about their values, missions, and passions, but when it comes right down to it, they struggle to make the sale or clinch the deals or produce the profit margins they want to deliver on expectations.

On the other hand, the drive mechanisms work perfectly. Let's say your bike has multiple gears and good traction and the tires are new. You can pedal easily, and the bike moves forward with power and speed. However, if the handlebars are crooked and the steering mechanism is loose, you will be unable to control your direction. You've got great engagement, but you are going very quickly in the wrong direction. A bike high on engagement but low on alignment is more than useless—it's dangerous.

Organizations high in engagement but low in alignment might get a lot done in short periods of time but will ultimately struggle with longevity because their core missions lack the sustainability to survive long-term. They accomplish goals quickly, but burnout, waste, and damaged relationships get in the way of accomplishing their overall goals.

Of course, if both wheels on the bicycle are unsound, with low alignment and low engagement, that is disintegration, which is the opposite of integrity. Organizations without alignment or engagement struggle to move forward at all. If entities in an organization are self-serving, mistrustful, or corrupt, organizations can "run themselves into the ground," much like riding a bike with structural and mechanical failures.

When a bicycle has structural integrity, all of the parts are aligned and can be engaged to do exactly what a bicycle is designed to do. When I use a mechanical metaphor for trust, what I really mean is that trust is structural. To speak of groups of human beings as functioning through "mechanics" is a bit simplistic; I use the bicycle model as a tool to illustrate the two sides of organizational integrity, which ultimately leads to "trust." In practical terms, trust is the outcome of organizational integrity – not limited to a personal characteristic.

For the purposes of this book, integration and integrity are essentially the same thing, coming from the word integral. When we talk about integrity, we're talking about the integration of alignment and engagement. When all dimensions and personnel in an organization are high in alignment and engagement, the mechanics of the organization work well.

Because trust is an outcome, it can be cultivated. By planting, nurturing, and harvesting organizational integrity at all levels of your organization you can increase your organization's ability to continue to grow and thrive. In high-trust organizations, each member relies on the other to invest time, talents, and effort into shared outcomes and goals. Integrating alignment with drive is one overarching structural change you can make to effectively revitalize your organization at all levels. As with most cultural dynamics, trust starts at the most basic level: the individual.

PRACTICES

PLAN

MISSION

VISION

VALUES

PRINCIPLES

PRACTICES

Assessing and Building Team Trust

As we learned with integrity, "trust" can be a tricky word—especially if incorrectly conflated with identifying as a "good" person. To accuse someone of not trusting or being untrustworthy can trigger deeply held beliefs about their own worth. It is important to distinguish our ability to earn trust, or to be 'trustworthy' from other's willingness to extend trust. Remember what we've discussed about the difference between influence and control. This is based on the principle of agency. We can't control whether others will trust us, we can be aware of the influence we're having on trust. This chapter is about how we, as leaders, build trust and create culture at the organizational level. At the individual level, trust is something that we hold dear; at the organizational level it drives the very fabric of daily living.

As Doug of Office Movers Association stressed to us, "[Trust is] really the number one thing. We named 2022 The Year of Trust with OMA and we spend an awful lot of time talking about that with professional speakers, coaches, etc. But at the end of the day, one of the things I remind everybody of was the very first thing, when there were six of us that got together, before it was even OMA, the very first things we all realized and knew we had to do was trust each other. That very beginning concept of OMA, 15, 16 years ago, of trusting each other, is still today the most paramount thing we have to do in our organization."

In building organizational integrity, think of trust as an outcome (the fruit of a well cultivated tree), not limited to a character trait, and cultivating it on the organizational level by assessing it at the individual level. Building trust is something that you will need to take very seriously, first by assessing your current level of trust in your organization(s) and then by developing an effective influence strategy to build on and appreciate high trust or overcome areas of low trust.

The rest of this chapter outlines an assessment tool you can use to identify the level of trust that you and your team have what you need to accomplish your shared mission and allow you to bolster it where necessary. Then, I provide suggestions for cultivating trust as a product (or "fruit") on your organizational tree.

To utilize this method, you need to understand the cause and effect that builds from principles, to values, to mission, to plans, to practices. Making the method work involves turning theory into practice. The tools that I outline in this section are tangible, practical solutions for organizations seeking to create a culture of integrity. In medicine, to prescribe without diagnosing is malpractice. That applies to leadership as well. Without assessing the needs of those you lead, it's impossible to know if you should coach, provide training or resources, or manage differently.

For over thirty years, I've worked with clients to help them build on their success as leaders. I've developed this tool to help them make the invisible visible. They are then able to move forward in areas where they were stuck or off track. Utilizing this tool will enable you to identify the causes of success and disappointments, understand the integration of alignment and engagement, create strategies for building trust, identify specific skills, traits, or behaviors that either contribute to or detract from healthy trust, assess sources of trust and mistrust, and address issues of trust by limiting defensiveness and increasing focus on stakeholder outcomes in your organization.

Assessment of Team Trust

Name	Values	Alignment		Engagement	
		Vision	Mission	Capabilities	Results
Definition:	Do the individual's values align with the values of the company, position, or the strategic priority?	Does the individual understand what success looks like?	Does the individual understand and align with the needs of all stakeholders?	Does this person have the time, talent, team and tools required to be successful?	Does this person consistently deliver expected results in a timely manner?
					(Effected by previous issues or management. Management includes plan, clear assignments,
Leader influence		*(Coaching: communicate hierarchy of consequences)*		*(training, structure, resources)*	*follow up and adaptation)*

To use this chart, list your team members or other stakeholders in the left-hand column, (including yourself). Use green for good-to-go; yellow for caution or needs work; and red for stalled or off track, in each area listed along the top. Then make a brief note identifying the strength or weakness in that area. You are familiar with most of these elements from previous chapters, but here is a brief refresher to assist you in applying the model. When assessing team members in each of these areas it is important to remember that you are not assessing people on whether they are a "good" or "bad" person. You are not bringing this to your team to say "Now I'll know how trustworthy you are." Instead, you are assessing them on how well they are equipped to fulfill each of these areas. In short, how much can they be trusted to be a contributing member of the group, based on how they have been prepared to align with organizational values, carry out collective missions, and utilize the available resources? This is not a tool to judge personality traits or characters. When you use this tool, you are essentially saying to your team "I want to go through this assessment and see what our needs are going to be, I want to identify our strengths and identify areas where I can improve in helping us to build trust." The bottom line: you're assessing your responsibility and opportunity to provide the influence and support your team needs to be successful.

In assessing the needs of the individual, determine if the person's values align with the values of the company, their role, or the strategic priority you are assessing. Remember, this is not limited to your opinion of how "good" this person is. It's about alignment. For example, there is nothing intrinsically wrong with the value of creativity, inspiration, or thinking "outside of the box." However, if the person is an accountant, "creative finance" is usually frowned upon and often illegal.

Vision and Mission refer to the person's understanding of what success will look like and who the stakeholders are, what they expect and his or her commitment to their outcomes.

Capabilities, in this case, refers to the person's ability to get the job done. Think in terms of Time, Talent, Tools, or Team. Does this person have the skills, the resources, and the support necessary for them to accomplish their part of the mission?

Outcomes have to do with meeting your organizational goals. If you or your team are limited in any of the three other areas (values, mission, or capabilities) then your ability to produce the outcomes you want will be limited. Even when those three areas are green, you may still find you are not getting the outcomes you expect. In this case you usually find your management style doesn't fit the individual or the situation.

To illustrate the purpose and usefulness of this chart, I've included several examples from my work experience to explain how leaders have used it to assess and develop the level of trust in their team and, ultimately, in their organization.

Values

For the purposes of the Team Trust Assessment, the Values category refers to a person's ability to understand, appreciate, and align with organizational values, which we have already covered in earlier chapters. For the most part, individuals tend to report alignment with values, for obvious reasons. People rarely will recognize or admit that they do not share values with those around them, which is why it is crucial to evaluate organizational values and team members' alignment with them.

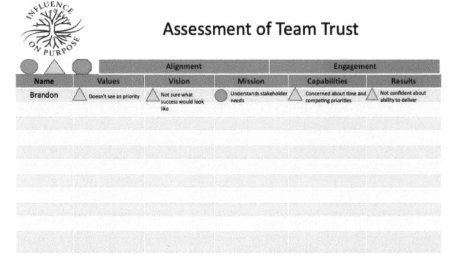

Assessment of Team Trust

| Name | Values | Alignment | | Engagement | |
		Vision	Mission	Capabilities	Results
Brandon	Doesn't see as priority	Not sure what success would look like	Understands stakeholder needs	Concerned about time and competing priorities	Not confident about ability to deliver

Occasionally, however, someone will recognize that what they value does not align with the rest of the group. While discussing a top priority in an organization, an executive (we'll call him Brandon), after some thought, spoke up and said, "You know what? I'm a yellow on values." I invited him to say more.

Brandon elaborated, "I understand that it's important to the team and I know that I have to get in alignment with it. I don't resent it, it's just that I've got so many things going on, I don't see this as a top priority. However, I know that it is because everyone else on the team sees it as one, so I'm all in, but I'm going to have to remember to keep it on my own priority list."

In Brandon's case, periodic coaching helped him remember that his team valued that particular outcome.

Vision

Vision is assuring the individual has a clear understanding of desired outcomes or what success will look like.

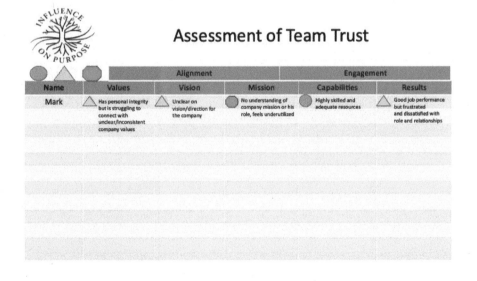

Assessment of Team Trust

Name				Alignment		Engagement	
Name	Values		Vision	Mission	Capabilities		Results
Mark	Has personal integrity but is struggling to connect with unclear/inconsistent company values		Unclear on vision/direction for the company	No understanding of company mission or his role, feels underutilized	Highly skilled and adequate resources		Good job performance but frustrated and dissatisfied with role and relationships

Mark is in a frustrating position. He is in the management team for a mid-sized company that is trying to grow from a startup to a more established enterprise. The levels and quality of leadership are changing as they try to support a larger, more layered structure. Unfortunately, in this important stage of growth, some of the things that have gotten lost are a common understanding of the company's values, vision, and mission. The company founders haven't clearly, consistently communicated these to their managers and as a result, Mark doesn't feel aligned to them or understand his role in accomplishing them. He is frustrated because his own high, personal drive to achieve and progress suffers from this misalignment and inability to successfully influence his environment. He wants to be a part of building something great but he's not sure if he's in the right place for that anymore. He feels underutilized and like he's stagnating in his current workplace, just checking boxes and treading water in a directionless situation. He is a skilled worker and has good management skills, so both he and his team are performing well, but his sense of being stuck and without direction leads to great personal dissatisfaction with his work and relationships with company leadership. For someone like Mark, it is just a matter of time before they begin looking for more fulfilling work and growth opportunities elsewhere. This is a danger of having unclear, inconsistent, or even non-existent company values, vision and mission.

Mission

Mission is all about understanding and committing to stakeholder needs and expectations. As mentioned earlier, a well-written mission encompasses the needs of all stakeholders in an organization, Team members should be familiar with stakeholder needs in order to meet those needs and foster those relationships.

Assessment of Team Trust

| | | Alignment | | | Engagement | |
Name	Values	Vision	Mission	Capabilities	Results
CEO	Priority is high in importance	Has a clear view of what is expected	Feel disconnected from stakeholder needs and expectations	Have the skills and resources required	Failure to align with stakeholders will compromise outcomes

In some cases, a person will feel disconnected from the stakeholders. I was working with an executive team using this tool to evaluate their readiness to take on the strategic priorities of their organization. As we came to one of the priorities, the CEO said, I have to give myself a yellow on Mission for this one. You could almost hear an audible gasp ripple through the room. She went on to explain that she had been leading the company for a couple of years and they had successfully turned around a number of urgent and important issues. This particular issue was important but had not been considered urgent. Her concern was that she had lost connection with the stakeholder's needs and expectation on that particular initiative. She gave herself the assignment to meet with stakeholders and understand their perspectives on the matter. This not only dramatically increased the likelihood of success for that strategic priority, it set a powerful example for the rest of the team.

Capabilities

As mentioned above, capabilities, as a category, refers to the skills and resources needed to effectively produce outcomes in an organization, although it is more complicated than just ensuring all employees have a working computer. What traits, skills, aptitudes, trainings, and other resources do your team members have at their disposal? The old adage about a chain being only as strong as its weakest link applies here. If any one of your team members is lacking in the resources needed to effectively do their job, your whole team will struggle. Although this might seem obvious at first, some of the deficiencies in this area could surprise you. For instance, I worked with a team member who said their team had no problem with follow through on their projects, but were experiencing communication issues with their assignments. Because they were unclear on what they needed to produce, they experienced setbacks and wasted time. To remedy situations like this, simply going back to clarify the mission can help. Just because someone has all the resources needed to accomplish their tasks does not mean they have all the needed capabilities.

Another important issue to consider for capabilities is the sharing of tasks. In the following example, let's say that co-worker Sue has been marked highly on all areas except for Capabilities. Sue's co-workers noted that she has "great work ethic and personal integrity" (Values), and "understands who the stakeholders are and that they have good relationships" (Mission), but was scored lower in Capabilities because she was spread too thin. Although Sue had plenty of skills, resources, and talents to accomplish her job well, the distribution of work in that team meant that Sue was overtaxing herself.

Assessment of Team Trust

Name	Values	Vision	Mission	Capabilities	Results
Sue	Great work ethic and personal integrity	Aligns with and is committed to the company vision	Understands stakeholder needs, good relationships	Very skilled, spread too thin	Tends to over promise or take on too much

Interestingly, Sue was one of the highest-ranking and most-trusted individuals on her team. The CFO of her company expressed a very high level of "trust" in Sue and saw her as the most likely successor to his position. When he went through this process, he was surprised that he identified specific concerns in any area. He was able to acknowledge that he had been having underlying concerns he hadn't been able to identify or recognize. This process helped him pinpoint that she didn't always follow through on the commitments she made. After going through the chart, he realized she was taking on too much work for herself. Sue had a great deal of personal confidence and drive that was leading her to make great strides in the organization, but her workload was not balanced. Her CFO quickly recognized one of the strongest members of his team was being set up for failure. He met with Sue and outlined his concerns. (Please remember here, the purpose of the tool is not to measure whether someone is "trustworthy." It is to identify effective influence strategies to help your team members develop sustainable success.) Working together, they were able to identify a plan that involved prioritization, delegation, and learning when to say no.

Assessment of Team Trust

| Name | Values | Alignment | | Engagement | |
		Vision	Mission	Capabilities	Results
Jamie	Good fit with company values	Strongly committed to the company vision	Understands stakeholder needs and connects well	Technology requires excessive manual input	Puts in the extra time and effort to deliver results

Jamie's chart reads almost all green, except for Capabilities. As I worked with Jamie's supervisor, I almost suggested to him that it is impossible to be green in Outcomes if there is a yellow or red in Capabilities. Certainly, if capabilities are at risk, it's going to affect your outcomes. Thankfully, I didn't try to control the situation (I had learned from experience). Instead, I said, "That's an interesting pattern, I wouldn't expect that. How do you think that happened?"

This leader said Jamie always delivered on expectations. She never missed a deadline. After thinking for a moment, he recognized his concern was with her workload. Jamie did not have the technology she needed to do her job well. Instead, she worked overtime to manually churn out the work she could do much faster if their technology and systems were up to date.

With this perspective, her leader was able to meet with her and identify his concerns, both for her and for the company. First, he recognized her effort and thanked her for her consistent great results. He told her of his respect for her work/life balance and his concern that her workload had become unreasonable and would lead to burnout.

The company was already in the process of making significant upgrades in their technology. Streamlining Jamie's workload was one of the many benefits anticipated in this project. However, the fear was these improvements would be too slow in coming.

Together, they were able to come up with a strategy to help bridge the gap until the upgrades came online. This included re-prioritizing Jamie's workload and bringing in temporary help for some of the tasks that didn't require her expertise. The leader also bought her a gift certificate for an evening out.

This example illustrates the systemic nature of trust in organizations. Even someone like Jamie, who we can trust to the hilt to be aligned with our values, mission, and even deliver on expectations, still requires the time, tools, team, and talent to prevent burnout. The question becomes: Do I trust that Jamie will be here a year from now or that she will continue to perform at her current level or higher?

Think about that for a second. Here was someone who was an excellent fit for the company, was very skilled, and consistently delivered expected results. Most of us as leaders might think: "If it ain't broke, don't fix it." In this case, becoming broke became highly predictable. When the first time the problem is noticed is after the employee gets burned out and either leaves the company or quits in place, it's often too late to implement a solution.

That is why regularly assessing the individual is fundamental in understanding the organization as a whole. Purposeful influence means leading with integrity at the systemic and individual level. You don't just ask "What does my team need?", but, "What does my team need now? What will they need in the future?"

Outcome

The Outcome section can be a little more complicated to interpret. It is not unusual to have green in all the preceding areas and still have a yellow or red in outcomes. However, more commonly a yellow or red in Outcomes may be a result of one of the previous areas being at risk. As I said before, any weaknesses in Values, Vision, Mission or Capabilities will have an effect on Outcomes sooner or later.

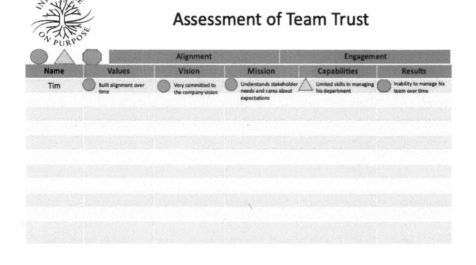

Assessment of Team Trust

Name	Values	Vision	Mission	Capabilities	Results
			Alignment		Engagement
Tim	Built alignment over time	Very committed to the company vision	Understands stakeholder needs and cares about expectations	Limited skills in managing his department	Inability to manage his team over time

One such case was with Tim. I met with a manager who led an individual who was green in the alignment categories, yellow in management skills (Capabilities), and red in Outcomes. When I asked about this, he responded that Tim had been with the company a long time. He was a great fit for company values, he understood and deeply cared about the stakeholders. He was beginning to manage others and was struggling with the responsibility. In this situation we found the level of management the leader was providing didn't fit Tim's needs. Tim was in a new role and needed more clarity on the plan, the assignment, and follow up and accountability. Tim's leader was used to him being very self-reliant and didn't want to "micro-manage" him. In essence, along with needing training on how to supervise others, Tim wasn't getting the management support he needed to get up to speed in his new role.

A little empathy goes a long way here. Can you image being Tim? You have been with a company you love for many years, you care deeply about those you serve, and you have a reputation for being a top performer. You get rewarded with a promotion and suddenly find yourself failing.

Being able to meet with Tim and identify needed training and the level of management support he needed to get up to speed allowed him to continue to grow and contribute to the success of the company.

Another possible pattern is that an individual will be strong in the first three areas, but still isn't getting the outcomes you would expect. If this is the case, then it's time to check your management strategies. Is the mission clear and does the plan address stakeholder expectations or needs? Have you made clear assignments in terms of who does what, by when? Have you identified an appropriate follow up strategy and are you creating accountability? Do you have a plan to evaluate and adapt your plan based on what you learned during execution? And are you giving your employees the support they need now? Effective coordination in these four areas helps you create a culture designed to accomplish your mission.

Assessment of Team Trust

| Name | Values | | Alignment | | Engagement | |
		Vision	Mission	Capabilities	Results
Ellie	No problem with company values or personal integrity	Motivated by the vision	Good understanding of expectations	Skills and resources adequate	Good follow through and accountability

The final example I'll use for this assessment is when you have the seemingly problem-free team member. Ellie appears to be the perfect employee, exactly who you want on your team. Her alignment and engagement are both green, she always delivers on her assignments: she's a "fire-and-forget" weapon. Again, it might seem reasonable to say, "If it ain't broke..." Some leaders might assume this is a case that requires nothing more from them. But there is danger in ignoring the "Ellies" of the team, in essentially taking them for granted.

I had a conversation about this very situation with a senior leader I worked with. I explained to him that Ellie is the person that we're most likely to overlook, and if she's not getting reinforcement at some point, she's going to start thinking "What the heck? Why do I even try?" He understood my point and added that Ellie is also the person that could easily be turned into a Sue if she's not given the support she needs. Remember, Sue was the team member who was very skilled and aligned with the team values and mission but was limited in capabilities because she was spread too thin, affecting her outcomes. Ellie is so good, the danger is that as her manager, I will keep giving her more to do because I know she will do it well. At some point I am going to overload her and then wonder what is wrong with her when she starts slipping, when her attitude starts to change or outcomes are affected. And I wouldn't know how to prevent this from happening if I wasn't looking at a chart like this and really evaluating "What does she need from me?" If this is my team, the first thing I'm going to notice is red. If that doesn't take all my attention, then I'm going to notice some of the yellows. I'm going to completely overlook Ellie if I'm not disciplined as a leader in spending time with each of my people and figuring out "What do they need now? What will they need next?" Most of us are familiar with the saying "the squeaky wheel gets the grease." However, a better saying may be "pay me now or pay me later;" or "An ounce of prevention is worth a pound of cure."

In my coaching, I use the analogy of meeting regularly with my children. Every month when my children were still at home, we'd have a Daddy-daughter or a Daddy-son meeting one-on-one. We'd sit down together and talk about the usual things: "how's life, how are you doing, etc?" I would also say "Is there anything that I need to do differently or better? Is there anything that I'm doing as your dad that's making it hard for you that I'm not aware of?" And almost always they would say "Oh, you're a good dad, you're doing fine." But every once in a while, one of them would give me a different answer.

For example, when my son was about seventeen and I asked him what I could do differently, he took a deep breath and said "Dad, there is one thing." I said "Really, what is it?" He said "I know that I make mistakes and I'm trying hard to get better. But every time I do something that I shouldn't, you act like it's all your fault, that somehow you let me down because I did something wrong. You taught me to own my own mistakes. I don't need that kind of pressure." And I said, "I get it. In a way, it's guilt tripping you. That wasn't my intention, I apologize." And I was able to say "I make you a promise: I will hold you accountable for your own choices, that's how you've been brought up and that's what I want to do. I get it. However, there is something you might not understand until you're a Dad. The things you do will always profoundly affect the people who love you. That's just how that's going to play out. I can't save you from that one." And he said "Ok, got it."

It's not always easy to tell someone in authority over you what they could or should be doing differently. It takes a good relationship, and it takes trust. Because I had regular meetings on an ongoing basis with my children, all of them felt they could talk to me about anything. That's why Bethany at thirty-something could call and tell me the details of a date that most young women wouldn't want to talk to their dad about. The same thing is true with your employees. Even though Ellie is green now, by meeting with her on a regular basis, when, not if, but when something comes up that's a problem for her, she's going to feel safe talking to me about it. If she gets the impression that I don't have time for her, if something comes up that's a problem, I don't have a clue how she's going to handle it. Odds are, she's not going to come to me with it. She's going to figure it out some other way, or it's just going to get worse and worse. The most important things to remember with Ellie are: one: don't dump on her, and two: keep those lines of communication open because things are going to change, that's a guarantee.

Don't overlook the Ellies in your organization: they are the regenerative ones, the ones that provide favorable outcomes that make the organization grow and thrive. Ellie is your opportunity. This was another point that came up while I was talking to Ellie's supervisor. He said, "She probably is the one who might start to get stale if we don't give her a chance to grow." She might be our next manager if she's a supervisor. She might be the next Vice President if she's a director. She is the future of the company. By meeting with her regularly, we can build a level of trust that can support her as she grows. That lets me be a leader who helps people develop and grow, and if I do that, then I am literally developing and growing the company. If I'm the leader who only focuses on fixing problems and treading water, then I'm a leader who's not developing and growing the company. I'm probably a good manager and not a very good leader, and I need to be both.

Start with Yourself

When using this assessment, I always recommend the leaders of the company or team start with themselves. As we saw in the case of the CEO who opened the doors of trust for everyone by being honest about her lack of connection with certain stakeholders, leadership involves vulnerability. Applying this model to myself helped me finally come to terms with writing this book. I've been told for years I should write a book but have always rejected the idea. Looking at our chart, I wasn't aligned with the idea. Though others saw it, I didn't feel I had anything to offer that wasn't already written (Values: red). I didn't see how others could be served by a book I would write (Mission: red). Even though I had written a few well-received articles, I wasn't sure how I would even go about writing a book (Capabilities: yellow). I had been told I needed to write a book for years and still had never written one (Outcomes: red). The result: no book.

As time passed and I continued to work with individuals and teams, I found these models made a difference. People who struggled to see the connection of values, vision, and mission with strategic planning and business outcomes were able to make those connections. Others found themselves able to address and influence situations and circumstances they had been blind to or had been avoiding in the past. *Maybe I should write a book*, I thought.

With this realization, I was able to go to green on Values, Vision and Mission. I was aligned with the idea of writing a book. This didn't help much on the engagement side of the equation. I was still a yellow on the how-to. Having never written a book and unsure on the process to even begin, I remained red on Outcomes.

What should I do? Ask for help! So, in a very real way, this book comes to you because I followed my own advice. As a leadership coach, I help successful people move to continued success at whatever level is next for them. Working with others helped me with both the process and the follow up (Accountability) I needed to actually get a book written.

Assessment of Team Trust

Name	Values	Vision	Mission	Capabilities	Results
		Alignment		**Engagement**	
John (before)	Didn't recognize any value in writing a book	Didn't know what a successful book would look like	Couldn't see how others would be benefited	Some success in writing articles etc. Not sure how to write a book.	Never wrote a book
John (years later)	Recognized value of my perspective	I could see what a successful book would look like	Positive results in people's businesses and in their lives	Not sure how the process works. Do research, get coaching	Make commitments and follow through on plans
John (now)	See the value of the models and the experience	I can see how those I serve would use the book.	Care deeply about the success of the people I serve	Learned a lot through the coaching, research and practice.	Here's your book. I hope it helps you Influence On Purpose

CONCLUSION

"... And the Greatest of These is Love" 1 Corinthians 13:13

I hope this conclusion serves more as a confirmation or reminder of the most important principle supporting regenerative leadership.

Many years ago, I was sitting in church listening to the speaker. Something that was said brought to mind something I had been considering regarding my work as an executive or leadership coach. I found many people struggle with the concept of authority. Some seek authority because of the feeling of accomplishment and power they feel it gives them. Others shun authority because they associate it with being controlling and with poor leadership they've experienced. As in many cases, these fight or flight mindsets miss the opportunity to contribute to a regenerative culture.

One dictionary defines authority as the power and right to give orders. The inspiration I received was to redefine 'authority' for the purpose of leadership in a regenerative culture, I define authority as 'authorized to serve.' By this I mean a person in a leadership position is authorized to serve others in accomplishing the mission of the organization. Think of what this means for you. When you were given (or earned) a certain job or title, you were granted authorization to serve that company, department, group or individual in accomplishing the mission that defined their work.

This brings us to a better understanding of stewardship. Stewardship is commonly understood to mean being assigned a surrogate role as a caretaker. This means what we are given authority to take care of is not something (or someone) we own. As a rancher, though I legally may own all or a portion of the land I manage, it will be there after I am gone. The question is: will I leave it better or worse than I found it? Similarly, the people I have stewardship for as a leader have a life and experience far beyond the influence I have as their leader. This includes my stewardship as an executive, as a father and husband, in my church calling, etc.

Over the years, I have continually been granted the opportunity to serve in our church. Some of those have been in the role of leader where I was assigned stewardship for the congregation in our area. I came to understand that for me, the greatest gift came with the greatest burden. That was as a steward or even shepherd for those people at that time. I was given the incredible gift to be able to feel at least a portion of God's love for those he called me to serve.

This means several things as I understand it. To feel God's love is to feel something of His joy and pain. I think of times in scripture when we get to see what brings joy to Jesus and times when he sorrowed and even wept.

As we align ourselves with God in our stewardships, we feel more intensely of both his joy and pain in the goodness and the suffering of those we serve. In this, we are receiving a gift from God in being a part of His work.

As a leadership coach, I often find myself working with those I serve to help them deal with difficult issues. These may include how to help an associate who is struggling; how to reinforce someone who is excelling and help them grow in their career; how to prepare for an important board presentation; how to work through a conflict with a peer. This ability to contribute to the tactical and strategic success of a client is important. However, it is not what is most important. As I act as a steward for those I serve, I understand my work is to help people be the leader they really want to be. It is to help them plant their roots in the principles that help them to cultivate a regenerative culture. One that nourishes the life and energy of the people they serve as steward and the organization they build and sustain.

ABOUT THE AUTHORS

John Baker is the Founder and Managing Partner of Influence On Purpose. He is a member of the Human Capital Institute and is a certified Master Human Capital Strategist. John has also served as the COO for Robinson Investments and as Chief Human Capital Officer and Director of Leadership Development and Executive Coaching at Sequent.

Rebekah Eyre is a Leadership and Executive coach with Influence On Purpose. As a former Staff Sergeant of the U.S. Marine Corps, Rebekah expertly led teams to achieve goals in stressful and complex environments. She's a shrewd manager of large-scale programs, as well as an accomplished advisor for senior leadership on adoption, training, and implementation of initiatives.